PENGUIN  LIBERTY

RELIGIOUS FREEDOM

Corey Brettschneider is a professor of political science at Brown University, where he teaches constitutional law and politics, as well as a visiting professor of law at Fordham University School of Law. He has also been a visiting professor at Harvard Law School and the University of Chicago Law School. His writing has appeared in *The New York Times*, *Politico*, and *The Washington Post*. He is the author of *The Oath and the Office: A Guide to the Constitution for Future Presidents*, two books about constitutional law and civil liberties, and numerous articles published in academic journals and law reviews. His constitutional law casebook is widely used in classrooms throughout the United States. Brettschneider holds a PhD in politics from Princeton University and a JD from Stanford Law School.

RELIGIOUS FREEDOM

A Selection

EDITED WITH AN INTRODUCTION BY
Corey Brettschneider

SERIES EDITOR
Corey Brettschneider

PENGUIN BOOKS

PENGUIN BOOKS
An imprint of Penguin Random House LLC
penguinrandomhouse.com

LIBRARY OF CONGRESS CATALOGING-IN-PUBLICATION DATA
Names: Brettschneider, Corey Lang, editor.
Title: Religious freedom / edited with an introduction by Corey Brettschneider.
Description: New York : First edition. | Penguin Books, 2021. |
Series: Penguin liberty | Includes bibliographical references.
Identifiers: LCCN 2021015476 (print) | LCCN 2021015477 (ebook) |
ISBN 9780143135142 (paperback) | ISBN 9780525506829 (ebook)
Subjects: LCSH: Freedom of religion—United States—History—Sources.
Classification: LCC KF4783 .R4283 2021 (print) | LCC KF4783 (ebook) |
DDC 342.7308/52—dc23
LC record available at https://lccn.loc.gov/2021015476
LC ebook record available at https://lccn.loc.gov/2021015477

Printed in the United States of America
1st Printing

Set in ACaslonPro
Designed by Daniel Lagin

Contents

RELIGIOUS FREEDOM

Part IV: RELIGIOUS FREEDOM AND DISCRIMINATION

Series Introduction

On November 9, 1989, the Berlin Wall fell. Two years later, in December 1991, the Soviet Union collapsed. These events, markers of the end of the Cold War, were seen by many as the final triumphant victory of democracy over authoritarianism and communism. Political scientist Francis Fukuyama famously declared the era to be the "end of history," suggesting that Western-style liberalism was the ultimate form of human ideology. There was a strong consensus—at least in the West—that liberal freedoms were necessary in any society.

But since then, that consensus has been shaken. In the twenty-first century, democracies have crumbled across the globe, with authoritarian leaders grabbing power and eroding traditional rights protections. Examples abound. Mexico and the Philippines embarked on extrajudicial drug wars; Nicolás Maduro's regime brought a state of near-famine to Venezuela; Poland's Law and Justice Party functionally turned parts of the media into its propaganda arm. In countless other countries, leaders have impinged on citizens' freedom. Even the United States—where liberal freedoms have often been taken for granted—has faced powerful movements and leaders who have disputed the legitimacy of the very rights that underpin our democracy.

Yet in the United States, calls to restrict rights have always run up against a powerful adversary, one that dates back to the country's founding: the Constitution of the United States. This Penguin Liberty series is designed to explore the Constitution's protections, illuminating how its text and values can help us as modern citizens to reflect on the meaning of liberty and understand how to defend it. With rights-based democracy under attack from all angles, it is crucial to engage in ongoing discussion about the meaning of liberty, its limits, and its role in the modern world.

Certainly, the ideal of liberty has been present in America since the dawn of the American Revolution, when Patrick Henry reportedly declared, "Give me liberty, or give me death!" In 1776, the Declaration of Independence proclaimed liberty an "unalienable Right"—along with "life" and the "pursuit of Happiness"—enshrining it as a central American aspiration.

These statements, however, are only a start in thinking about liberty. Mistakenly, they seem to suggest that liberty is absolute, never limited. But in this series, we will see that idea continually challenged. Various liberties sometimes conflict, and we must deliberate among them. Importantly, the liberty to be free from government intervention, or what the British philosopher Isaiah Berlin called "negative liberty," must sometimes be balanced against our liberty as a democratic people to govern in the general interest, an idea he called "positive liberty." Thus, the series will also emphasize the importance of liberty not only in terms of freedom from government intervention, but also as self-government, the freedom of all of us collectively to decide on our own destinies.

Ratified in 1788, the Constitution was an attempt to codify the high ideal of liberty as self-government. Through intense debate at the Constitutional Convention, a document was forged that limited government power and gave people a say in how they were to be governed. Its goal was to "secure the Blessings of Liberty to ourselves and our Posterity." Still, many Americans were not convinced the Constitution went far enough in protecting their individual freedom from government coercion—what Berlin would call "negative liberty." Although the push for a Bill of Rights failed at the Constitutional Convention, the First Congress ratified one in 1791. These first ten amendments to the Constitution focused largely on securing individual liberties.

Just over 4,500 words long when originally passed, the U.S. Constitution is the shortest written governing charter of any major democracy. Its brevity belies its impact. Ours is the world's longest surviving written constitution. Some scholars estimate that, at one time, as many as 160 other nations based their constitution at least in part on the U.S. Constitution. The United Nations Universal Declaration of Human Rights from 1948 overlaps significantly with provisions of our Bill of Rights. Individual freedoms that our Constitution champions inspire peoples across the globe.

Of course, the original Constitution protected liberty for only a restricted few. As written in 1787, the Constitution did not explicitly outlaw racialized chattel slavery. Almost 700,000 black people were enslaved in the United States at the time of its founding, a fact that the Constitution did nothing to change and tacitly allowed. Article I prohibited Congress from outlawing the international slave trade until 1808, and the three-fifths clause cemented Southern white political power by having enslaved people count toward political representation without allowing them to vote.

Not all the framers wanted the Constitution to be tainted by slavery. James Madison and Alexander Hamilton, for example, thought slavery morally wrong. But they were willing to compromise this conviction in order for Southern states to ratify the document they so cherished. Thus was born America's original sin, a legally sanctioned system of racial oppression that persisted formally until the Civil War. Only after an estimated more than 600,000 Americans gave their lives in that bloody conflict was the Constitution amended to outlaw slavery, guarantee "equal protection of the laws," and establish that race could deny no citizen access to the franchise.

Enslaved Americans were not the only ones left out of the original Constitution's promise of liberty. Women were guaranteed no formal rights under the Constitution, and they were deprived of equal political status until 1920, when suffragists finally succeeded in amending the Constitution to guarantee women the vote. In the Founding Era, the vote in many states was restricted mainly to white male property owners.

These significant failures are reasons to criticize the Constitution. But they should not lead anyone to discount it altogether. First, the Constitution has demonstrated a remarkable resilience and capacity for change. In each of the cases described above, the Constitution was later amended to attempt to rectify the wrong and expand citizens' rights. Second, and perhaps more important, the Constitution's deepest values have often inspired and strengthened the hand of those seeking justice. That's why Frederick Douglass, himself a former enslaved person, became an ardent supporter of the Constitution, even before the passage of the post–Civil War amendments that ended slavery and provided equal rights. In his Fourth of July oration in 1852, he praised the Constitution as a "glorious liberty document" but added a crucial caveat: it protected liberty only when it was "interpreted as it ought to be interpreted." Douglass believed that while many saw the Constitution as a pro-slavery document, its text and values supported broad protections for freedom and equality.

Douglass's point, though delivered more than 150 years ago, inspires this Penguin Liberty series. The Constitution is not a static document. Nor is it just a set of provisions on paper. The Constitution is a legal document containing specific rules, but it also gives voice to a broader public morality that transcends any one rule.

What exactly that public morality stands for has always been up for debate and interpretation. Today, after the passage of the post–Civil War amendments, the Constitution takes a clear stand against racial subordination. But there are still many other vital questions of liberty on which the Constitution offers guidance without dictating one definite answer. Through the processes of interpretation, amendment, and debate, the Constitution's guarantees of liberty have, over time, become more fully realized.

In these volumes, we will look to the Constitution's text and values, as well as to American history and some of its most important thinkers, to discover the best explanations of our constitutional ideals of liberty. Though imperfect, the Constitution can be the country's guiding light in dark times, illuminating a path to the recovery of liberty. My hope is that these volumes offer readers the chance to hear the strongest defenses of constitutional ideals, gaining new (or renewed) appreciation for values that have long sustained the nation.

No single fixed or perfectly clear meaning of the Constitution will emerge from this series. Constitutional statements of liberty are often brief, open to multiple interpretations. Competing values within the document raise difficult questions, such as how to balance freedom and equality, or privacy and security. I hope that as you learn from the important texts in these volumes, you undertake a critical examination of what liberty means to you—and how the Constitution should be interpreted to protect it. Though the popular understanding may be that the Supreme Court is the final arbiter of the Constitution, constitutional liberty is best protected when not just every branch of government but also every citizen is engaged in constitutional interpretation. Questions of liberty affect both our daily lives and our country's values, from what we can say to whom we can marry, how society views us to how we determine our leaders. It is Americans' great privilege that we live under a Constitution that both protects our liberty and allows us to debate what that liberty should be.

The central features of constitutional liberty are freedom and equality, values that are often in tension. One of the Constitution's most important declarations of freedom comes in the First Amendment, which provides that "Congress shall make no law respecting an establishment of religion, or prohibiting the free exercise thereof; or abridging the freedom of speech, or of the press; or the right of the people peaceably to assemble, and to petition the Government for a redress of grievances." And one of its most important declarations of equality comes in the Fourteenth Amendment, which reads in part, "no State shall . . . deny to any person within its jurisdiction the equal protection of the laws." These Penguin Liberty volumes look in depth at these conceptions of liberty while also exploring what mechanisms the Constitution has to protect its guarantees of liberty.

Freedom of speech provides a good place to begin to explore the Constitution's idea of liberty. It is a value that enables both the protection of liberty and the right of citizens to debate its meaning. Textually, the constitutional guarantee that Congress cannot limit free speech might read as though it is absolute. Yet for much of U.S. history, free speech protections were minimal. In 1798, President John Adams signed the

Sedition Act, essentially making it a crime to criticize the president or the U.S. government. During the Civil War, President Abraham Lincoln had some dissidents and newspapers silenced. In 1919, a moment came that seemed to protect free speech, when Justice Oliver Wendell Holmes wrote in *Schenck v. United States* that speech could be limited only when it posed a "clear and present danger." But, in fact, this ruling did little to protect free speech, as the Court repeatedly interpreted danger so broadly that minority viewpoints, especially leftist viewpoints, were often seen as imprisonable.

Today, however, U.S. free speech protections are the most expansive in the world. All viewpoints are allowed to be expressed, except for direct threats and incitements to violence. Even many forms of hate speech and opinions attacking democracy itself—types of speech that would be illegal in other countries—are generally permitted here, in the name of free expression. The Court's governing standard is annunciated in *Brandenburg v. Ohio*, which protects vast amounts of speech as long as that speech does not incite "imminent lawless action." How did we get from the Sedition Act to here?

Two thinkers have played an outsize role: John Stuart Mill and Alexander Meiklejohn. Mill's 1859 classic, *On Liberty,* is an ode to the idea that both liberty and truth will thrive in an open exchange of ideas, where all opinions are allowed to be challenged. In this "marketplace of ideas," as Mill's idea has often come to be called, the truth stays vibrant instead of decaying or descending into dogma. Mill's idea explains the virtue of free speech and the importance of a book series about liberty: Challenging accepted ideas about what liberty is helps bring the best ideas to light. Meiklejohn's theory focuses more on the connection between free speech and democracy. To him, the value of free speech is as much for the listeners as it is for the speakers. In a democracy, only when citizens hear all ideas can they come to informed conclusions about how society should be governed. And only informed citizens can fully exercise other democratic rights besides speech, like the right to vote. Meiklejohn's insistence that democratic citizens need a broad exposure to ideas of liberty inspires this series.

Freedom of religion is another central constitutional value that allows citizens the liberty to be who they are and believe what they wish. It is enshrined in the First Amendment, where the Establishment Clause prevents government endorsement of a religion and the Free Exercise Clause gives citizens the freedom to practice their religion. Though these two religion clauses are widely embraced now, they were radically new at the time of the nation's founding. Among the first European settlers in America were the Puritans, members of a group of English Protestants who were persecuted for their religion in their native Britain. But colonial America did not immediately and totally embrace religious toleration. The Church of England still held great sway in the South during the colonial era, and many states had official religions—even after the Constitution forbade a national religion. At the time the Constitution was ratified, secular government was a rarity.

But religious tolerance was eventually enshrined into the U.S. Constitution, thanks in large part to the influence of two thinkers. British philosopher John Locke opposed systems of theocracy. He saw how government-imposed religious beliefs stifled the freedom of minority believers and imposed religious dogma on unwilling societies. In the United States, James Madison built on Locke's ideas when he drafted the First Amendment. The Free Exercise Clause protected the personal freedom to worship, acknowledging the importance of religious practice among Americans. But on Madison's understanding, the Establishment Clause ensured against theocratic imposition of religion by government. Doing so respected the equality of citizens by refusing to allow the government to favor some people's religious beliefs over others'.

A more explicit defense of equality comes from the Equal Protection Clause of the Fourteenth Amendment. But as our volume on the Supreme Court shows, the Constitution has not always been interpreted to promote equality. Before the Civil War, African Americans had few, if any, formal rights. Millions of African American people were enslaved, and so-called congressional compromises maintained racial subordination long after the importation of slaves was banned in 1808. A burgeoning abolitionist movement gained moral momentum in the North, though the institution of slavery persisted. Liberty was a myth for enslaved people, who were unable to move freely, form organizations, earn wages, or participate in politics.

Still, the Supreme Court, the supposed protector of liberty, for decades failed to guarantee it for African Americans. And in its most notorious ruling it revealed the deep-seated prejudices that had helped to perpetuate slavery. Chief Justice Roger Taney wrote in the 1857 decision in *Dred Scott v. Sandford* that African Americans were not citizens of the United States and "had no rights which the white man was bound to respect." Taney's words were one spark for the Civil War, which, once won by the Union, led to the passage of the Thirteenth, Fourteenth, and Fifteenth Amendments. By ending slavery, granting citizenship and mandating equal legal protection, and outlawing racial discrimination in voting, these Reconstruction Amendments sought to reverse Taney's heinous opinion and provide a platform for advancing real equality.

History unfortunately shows us, however, that legal equality did not translate into real equality for African

Americans. Soon after Reconstruction, the Court eviscerated the Fourteenth Amendment's scope, then ruled in 1896 in *Plessy v. Ferguson* that racial segregation was constitutional if the separate facilities were deemed equal. This paved the way for the legally sanctioned institution of Jim Crow segregation, which relegated African Americans to second-class citizenship, denying them meaningful social, legal, and political equality. Finally, facing immense pressure from civil rights advocates including W. E. B. Du Bois and A. Philip Randolph, as well as the powerful legal reasoning of NAACP lawyer Thurgood Marshall, the Court gave the Equal Protection Clause teeth, culminating in the landmark 1954 *Brown v. Board of Education* decision, which declared that separate is "inherently unequal." Even after that newfound defense of constitutional equality, however, racial inequality has persisted, with the Court and country debating the meaning of liberty and equal protection in issues as varied as affirmative action and racial gerrymandering.

While the Fourteenth Amendment was originally passed with a specific intention to end racial discrimination, its language is general: "No State shall . . . deny to any person within its jurisdiction the equal protection of the laws." Over time, that generality has allowed civil rights advocates to expand the meaning of equality to include other groups facing discrimination. One significant example is the fight for gender equality.

Women had been left out of the Constitution; masculine pronouns pepper the original document, and women are not mentioned. In an 1807 letter to Albert Gallatin, Thomas Jefferson—the person who had penned the Declaration of Independence—wrote that "the appointment of a woman to office is an innovation for which the public is not prepared, nor am I." Liberty was a myth for many women, who were supposed to do little outside the home, had limited rights to property, were often made to be financially dependent on their husbands, and faced immense barriers to political participation.

Nevertheless, women refused to be shut out of politics. Many were influential in the burgeoning temperance and abolition movements of the nineteenth century. In 1848, Elizabeth Cady Stanton wrote the Declaration of Sentiments, amending the Declaration of Independence to include women. Still, suffragists were left out when the Fifteenth Amendment banned voting discrimination based on race—but not on gender. Only after Alice Paul and others led massive protests would the freedom to vote be constitutionally guaranteed for women through the Nineteenth Amendment.

Voting secured one key democratic liberty, but women were still denied the full protection of legal equality. They faced discrimination in the workplace, laws based on sexist stereotypes, and a lack of reproductive autonomy. That's where our volume on Supreme Court justice Ruth Bader Ginsburg begins. Now a feminist icon from her opinions on the Court, Justice Ginsburg earlier served as a litigator with the ACLU, leading their Women's Rights Project, where she helped to convince the Court to consider gender as a protected class under the Fourteenth Amendment. As a justice, she continued her pioneering work to deliver real gender equality, knowing that women would never enjoy the full scope of constitutional liberty unless they held the same legal status as men.

Ginsburg's work underscores how the meaning of constitutional liberty has expanded over time. While the Declaration of Independence did explicitly reference equality, the Bill of Rights did not. Then, with the Reconstruction Amendments, especially the Equal Protection Clause, the Constitution was imbued with a new commitment to equality. Now the document affirmed that democratic societies must protect both negative liberties for citizens to act freely and positive liberties for all to be treated as equal democratic citizens. Never has this tension between freedom and equality been perfectly resolved, but the story of our Constitution is that it has often inspired progress toward realizing liberty for more Americans.

Progress has been possible not just because of an abstract constitutional commitment to liberty, but also due to formal mechanisms that help us to guarantee it. Impeachment is the Constitution's most famous—and most explosive—way to do so. With the abuses of monarchy in mind, the framers needed a way to thwart tyranny and limit concentrated power. Borrowing in language and spirit from the British, who created a system of impeachment to check the power of the king, they wrote this clause into the Constitution: "The President . . . shall be removed from Office on Impeachment for, and Conviction of, Treason, Bribery, or other high Crimes and Misdemeanors."

Early drafts suggested grounds for impeachment should be just "treason or bribery." But George Mason and other delegates objected, wanting impeachable offenses to include broader abuses of power, not just criminal actions. Though Mason's original suggestion of "maladministration" was rejected, the ultimate language of "high Crimes and Misdemeanors" made it possible to pursue impeachment against leaders who threatened the Constitution's deeper values. Impeachment would stand as the ultimate check on officials who have overstepped their constitutional authority.

The House has formally impeached twenty officials throughout American history, and many more have faced some kind of impeachment inquiry. Most of those accused have been federal judges. Just five impeachment proceedings have reached the presidency, the highest echelon of American government. Andrew Johnson and Bill Clinton were each formally impeached once and Donald Trump was formally impeached twice, though none of these presidents were convicted and removed from office. Richard Nixon resigned after the House Judiciary Committee voted to impeach, before the full House vote could take place. Most of these impeachment proceedings had a background context in which a president was thought to have violated fundamental constitutional liberties—even if that violation was not always the primary component of the impeachment hearings themselves.

For Johnson, although his impeachment focused on the Tenure of Office Act, an underlying issue was his violation of the liberty of newly freed African Americans to live in society as equals. For Nixon, the impeachment inquiry focused on the Watergate break-in and cover-up, which threatened the liberty of voters to have fair elections and to hold their presidents criminally accountable. For Clinton, who was accused of perjury and obstruction of justice related to a sexual affair with a White House intern, critics argued that his flouting of criminal laws threatened the standard of equal justice under law—a standard necessary for democratic self-government. For Trump, the impeachment articles in his first trial accused him of soliciting foreign interference as an abuse of power—threatening the liberty of voters to have fair elections; and his second impeachment trial accused him of inciting an insurrection to prevent the peaceful transfer of power between administrations, threatening that previously uninterrupted hallmark of American democracy. Often, legalistic questions of criminal wrongdoing dominated these impeachment discussions, but concerns about violations of constitutional liberty were frequently present in the background.

While impeachment is an important remedy for presidential

abuse of liberty, liberty lives best when it is respected before crises arise. To do so requires that liberty not be relegated to an idea just for the purview of courts; rather, citizens and officials should engage in discussions about the meaning of liberty, reaffirming its centrality in everyday life.

By few people are those discussions better modeled than by the example of the now hip-hop famous Alexander Hamilton, a founding father and the nation's first secretary of the treasury. Hamilton was a prolific writer, and in our volumes we'll see him square off against other founders in debates on many major challenges facing the early republic. Against Samuel Seabury, Hamilton rejected the British colonial system and said liberty must come through independence. Against Thomas Jefferson (in an argument now immortalized as a Broadway rap battle), Hamilton advocated for a national bank, believing that a modern, industrial economy was needed to grow the nation. Against James Madison, he pushed for stronger foreign policy powers for the president.

The specifics of Hamilton's debates matter. His ideas shaped American notions of government power, from self-determination to economic growth to international engagement. He was instrumental in ratifying the very Constitution that still protects our liberties today. But just as important as *what* he argued for was *how* he argued for it. Hamilton thought deeply about what liberty meant to him, and he engaged in thoughtful, reasoned discussions with people he disagreed with. He cared both for his own freedoms and for the country's welfare at large.

My goal is for readers of these Penguin Liberty volumes to emulate Hamilton's passion for defending his ideas—even, or especially, if they disagree with him on what liberty means. Everyday citizens are the most important readers of this series—and the most important Americans in the struggle to protect and expand constitutional liberty. Without pressure from the citizenry to uphold constitutional ideals, elected leaders can too easily scrap them. Without citizens vigorously examining the meaning of liberty, its power could be lost. Left untended, the flames of liberty could quietly burn out.

The writings in these Penguin Liberty volumes are intended to give citizens the tools to contest and explore the meaning of liberty so it may be kept alive. None of the selections are simple enough to be summed up in tweets or dismissed with quick insults. They are reasoned, thoughtful attempts to defend constitutional ideals of liberty—or warnings about what can happen when those liberties are disregarded. The Constitution's guarantees of liberty have always been aspirations, not realized accomplishments. Yet if these volumes and other constitutional writings inspire us to bring discussions to dinner tables, classrooms, and workplaces across the country, they will be contributing to making those high ideals more real.

COREY BRETTSCHNEIDER

Introduction

The First Amendment of the U.S. Constitution states that "Congress shall make no law respecting an establishment of religion or prohibiting the free exercise thereof." Here, religious freedom is codified through two clauses, the Free Exercise Clause and the Establishment Clause. At first glance, the First Amendment's goal to protect freedom of religion appears uncontroversial. However, when we closely examine the First Amendment's impact on the regulation of religious practices, we can see that it remains one of the most contentious parts of the Constitution in both the political and judicial spheres of government in the United States.

The Free Exercise Clause feels familiar and logical to many. It would feel inconsistent with the American creed to allow government to ban people from worshipping as they choose, even if only a minority of people in the country practice the religion or the religion itself is unpopular. However, as with many issues of religious freedom, the meaning of "prohibiting" is rife with potential contention. Does it mean, as Justice Antonin Scalia has argued, that government in general cannot *intentionally* or *explicitly* limit religious practice? Or does it mean, as other justices have argued, that those whose religious practice was adversely affected by laws, even laws with nondiscriminatory intents, are entitled to protections under the First Amendment?

The Establishment Clause is based on an equally important and, in some ways, more complicated idea of religious freedom. Its clearest meaning is that Congress cannot establish an official church of the United States. The clause also prohibits laws that are related to establishing a religion, including those that would unduly promote some religions over others. The principle behind the Establishment Clause is sometimes called, following a phrase used in a letter by Thomas Jefferson, the "separation of church and state," but as we will see, no clear line divides these two spheres. For instance, the Supreme Court has repeatedly held that some public prayers and some religious displays on public property are constitutional, and it has held that some indirect and direct funding of religious institutions is constitutional. As a matter of law, the question is not whether any mixing of church and state is legal, but rather what kinds are legal—a line that has repeatedly proven difficult to draw.

In this volume, to understand the most pressing issues surrounding religious liberty, we turn to influential philosophical ideas about religious freedom that date from before the United States' founding to the present day. Using key cases from the Supreme Court, we will consider the limits of free exercise as well as the intersections of religious freedom with other civil liberties. And we will ask how these twin pillars of religious freedom—free exercise and the limit on religious establishment—unfold in daily life. In examining these readings and cases, my hope—as it is with all the volumes in this series—is that readers will come away not just with an appreciation of the history and current status of the law of religious freedom, but also with their own understanding of what the guarantee of religious freedom requires of our society.

A relevant place to begin an exploration of religious liberty is a landmark case on free exercise that reached the Supreme Court in 1992. *Church of the Lukumi Babalu Aye v. City of Hialeah* tested the legality of an ordinance passed by the city council of Hialeah, Florida, that banned animal sacrifice. As the case showed, the city council's decision to pass the ordinance was no mere coincidence. Hialeah was notably home to followers of the Santeria religion, which used animal sacrifices as a form of religious ceremony. This practice offended other community members in Hialeah. During city council meetings, where participants discussed the possibility of banning animal sacrifice, many did not mince words when voicing their discomfort with the Santeria community. In a resolution presaging the ordinance, the city alluded to Santeria's practices as "inconsistent with public morals, peace, or safety."

But the ordinance was soon struck down, as the Supreme Court ruled that it violated the First Amendment's Free Exercise Clause. According to the Supreme Court, the Hialeah ordinance constituted an intentional attempt by the council to limit the free exercise privileges of Santeria followers. In other words, the council's decision to pass the ordinance exemplified the kind of lawmaking that the Constitution's First Amendment explicitly forbids.

Although the Court ruled on free exercise, the case also raised interesting questions about the Establishment Clause. Supporters of the ordinance had suggested that Santeria was not a true church or religion. Such discourse could have been used to support a second argument against the constitutionality of the ordinance—that the Santeria religion as a whole was being degraded by a public law, in violation of the prohibition on the establishment of religion.

To understand the ban on establishment more clearly, it is helpful to examine the legal tradition that the framers sought to break away from. In Great Britain, the Church of England held a position of paramount importance, and it was the official state church of England. When drafting and ratifying the Constitution, the framers rejected the possibility of creating an official Church of the United States. Instead, they enshrined a limit on religious authority in the Constitution. Crucially, however, the framers did not just ban the establishment of a national church. The Establishment Clause also restricts laws "respecting" or related to an establishment of religion, so Congress cannot enact laws that improperly favor one religion over others.

In the Foundations section, we discuss the meaning of the Establishment Clause and Free Exercise Clause independently, but also in terms of their fit with one another. To understand these two clauses, a good place to start is with the philosophy of James Madison, who was the primary drafter of the First Amendment's language. At the Constitutional Convention in Philadelphia, Madison actually opposed the explicit protection of religious freedom and rejected the inclusion of a bill of rights in the Constitution. Madison argued that if rights were enumerated in the Constitution, that would reduce the vast protection of religious freedom he thought Americans were owed, because future governments might read those specifically defined protections narrowly rather than broadly. So, he argued, better not to give jurists language that could be abused to lessen rights protections. Eventually, he changed his mind. Under pressure from those seeking more explicit protections, Madison agreed to push for a substantive Bill of Rights in the first Congress. As an elected representative from Virginia, Madison drafted and contributed to the passage of the current First Amendment, with protections of religious freedom front and center.

Madison had a long history of arguing that there was a close link between free exercise and the limits on government's role in religious life. In a 1785 letter addressed to Virginia's General Assembly titled "Memorial and Remonstrance against Religious Assessments," he outlined his views on religious freedom. Madison wrote the piece in response to a tax proposed by the Virginia legislature that would fund "teachers of the Christian religion," including by provisioning some monies to churches. Madison argued that the tax elevated one religion over all the others. Madison also argued that the tax wrongly forced citizens to be associated with beliefs they did not necessarily share, directly limiting the concept of free exercise and blurring the important distinction between church and state.

Although Madison's belief in the limits on establishment broke with the British tradition, he drew inspiration for his views on religious freedom from the ideas of English philosopher John Locke. Specifically, Locke's "A Letter Concerning Toleration," explored in this volume, influenced Madison, and by extension the U.S. Constitution. Locke's letter remains a premier statement of the critical importance of religious freedom in the Western philosophical tradition.

Locke does not explicitly use the terms "free exercise" or "establishment" of religion in his letter, but his words illustrate why these two concepts cohere. In Locke's view, if the reasons for law are entirely theistic and have no secular rationale, government will inevitably favor one religion so strongly that it will limit the rights of members of other religions. The letter is thus an inspiration for thinking about the limit on establishment and free exercise as interrelated concepts.

In addition to Locke and Madison, we examine another thinker, Roger Williams, who provides an additional justification for both free exercise and the separation of church and state. Writing in 1644 from Rhode Island, Williams authored "A Plea for Religious Liberty." In this work, Williams illustrates a danger of mixing religion and government. In Williams's view, when the religious and secular are combined, religion itself is corrupted.

Alongside the words of Locke, Williams, and Madison, this volume includes the 1786 "Virginia Statute for Religious Freedom" by Thomas Jefferson, which deeply influenced the First Amendment of the U.S. Constitution. By section's end, readers will be familiar with key framers' beliefs on religious freedom in the United States.

The Foundations section celebrates the philosophical underpinnings of the twin ideals of religious freedom—free exercise and the ban on religious establishment. However, an exploration of the importance of religious freedom cannot end with theory. Since the First Amendment's ratification, its religion clauses have been subject to some of the most contentious cases in the Supreme Court's history. In subsequent sections of this volume, we examine these historic legal debates over religious liberty, alongside literature and speeches from key political figures in American history. The words and ideas of leaders, from George Washington to Barack Obama, and of influential Supreme Court justices, outline the central role that religion has played and continues to play in American life.

Although the Constitution maintains a boundary between government and religion, presidents such as George Washington and Thomas Jefferson have maintained respectful correspondence with religious communities across the United States. Their relationships with these communities illustrate an awareness that faith held enormous importance among American citizens—and this is still the case.

With the recognition that faith cannot be ignored, how must lawmakers address the religious needs and concerns of their constituents without violating the Establishment Clause? The responsibility of adjudicating this balance has repeatedly fallen to the Supreme Court. In this volume's section on Church and State, we will explore key Supreme Court cases, such as *Lemon v. Kurtzman, Lynch v. Donnelly*, and *American Legion v. American Humanist Association*, that track the development of the Court's thinking on the line between church and state. Readers will grapple with the facts of these cases and with various justices' approaches to them. You will see broad approaches, such as Justice Sandra Day O'Connor's, limiting laws that express "endorsement" of religion, and you will also see narrower ones, such as Justice Anthony Kennedy's emphasis on allowing religious displays and prayers as long as they do not "coerce" observers.

This volume also devotes a section to significant Supreme Court cases that resolved clashes over the Free Exercise Clause of the First Amendment. As you will read, the Court often has to identify the limits of the Free Exercise Clause in a variety of areas. For instance, can an employee be denied unemployment benefits after having been fired for refusing to work on Saturday when she celebrates the Sabbath on that day? Can another employee be denied unemployment benefits after having been fired for using peyote as part of a

Native American religious ritual? By the volume's end, readers will have a better sense of where they stand on these pressing questions.

Recent Supreme Court cases also touch on the interactions between the First Amendment and other fundamental civil rights and liberties. These cases have often forced the Court to mediate between allegations of discrimination and religious freedom violations. For instance, in *Masterpiece Cakeshop, Ltd. v. Colorado Civil Rights Commission* (2018), we examine a baker's claim that he has a free exercise right to refuse to bake a cake for a same-sex couple's wedding due to his religious convictions, despite Colorado's antidiscrimination statute that prohibits the denial of services to people because of their sexual orientation. Although the Supreme Court ultimately narrowly decided in favor of the baker, a debate rages on. While some worry about religious freedom claims interfering with the protection of civil rights, others argue the Court should be even more robust in defending religious freedom.

Another dire and pressing controversy over religious freedom came in *Trump v. Hawaii* (2018), which addressed the question of whether President Donald Trump's ban on travel to the United States from a number of countries with significant Muslim populations violated the Establishment Clause. As a group of colleagues and I argued in a brief excerpted in this volume, which was cosigned by more than forty-five legal scholars, the motive behind the president's ban was an unconstitutional animus toward Muslims. Just as discrimination against Santeria followers and against the cake shop owner violates the Free Exercise Clause, so too, we posited in a related argument, an attempt to ban a person's entry to the country based on religion is a violation of the Establishment Clause. While Justice Sonia Sotomayor quoted our brief in her dissent, the Supreme Court's majority disagreed with us. In its view, religious freedom guarantees those within our borders robust protections but does not offer that same level of protection to noncitizen civilians outside of the United States. The decision in *Trump v. Hawaii* and the opposing arguments laid out in our brief should prompt Americans to ask about the extent to which American religious freedom has been used to protect all religions, not just religions whose practitioners are in this country's majority.

As you read these cases, you will find that the Supreme Court rarely offers unanimous rulings in cases concerning the limits of the two religious clauses. Justices often walk away from the same case with vastly different views. For instance, in an excerpt of the case *Town of Greece v. Galloway* (2014), the justices considered whether the inclusion of a voluntary public prayer before a town meeting violated the Constitution's Establishment Clause. Writing for the majority, Justice Anthony Kennedy argued that the prayer's noncoercive nature saved it from violating the Constitution. In his dissent, Justice Stephen Breyer emphasized that the town's favoritism of Christian over non-Christian prayers constituted an unequal treatment of religions in violation of the Establishment Clause. Ultimately, the Supreme Court's lack of consensus and the diversity of opinions that it offers on religious liberty cases underscore the yet-to-be-resolved limits of the First Amendment's religion clauses.

From the founding to this day, debate has raged about both religion clauses. These readings are meant to help readers engage with the questions underlying the debate. Through this volume, you will be presented with arguments that allow you to form a sense of where you stand, for example, on the extent to which the Free Exercise Clause protects religious people and entitles them to be exempt from otherwise valid laws.

And you will have an understanding of what it means to pass a law that "respects" an establishment of religion. As with all the volumes of Penguin Liberty, my aim is not to offer or advance one perspective on the key liberty of religious freedom. Rather, I aim to use these texts and cases to stimulate debate among citizens and empower them to use the ideas of some of the greatest political and legal thinkers of our country's history who grappled with issues that we still face today.

COREY BRETTSCHNEIDER

A Note on the Text

All the works in this selection are excerpted, except for "The Virginia Statute," by Thomas Jefferson, "Letter to Touro Synagogue," by George Washington, "Letter to the Danbury Baptists," by Thomas Jefferson, "Veto Message on Incorporating the Alexandria Protestant Episcopal Church" and "Veto Message on Act of Relief for the Baptist Church," by James Madison, and "Islam Is Peace," by George W. Bush. Spelling and punctuation are kept as in the original. Footnotes have been eliminated from the text without marking. All works are in the public domain and can be found within the "Unabridged Source Materials" section in this book.

RELIGIOUS FREEDOM

Part I

FOUNDATIONS
of
RELIGIOUS FREEDOM

"A Plea for Religious Liberty," by *Roger Williams* (1644)

Roger Williams, a minister, was expelled from the Massachusetts Bay Colony for advocating religious tolerance and challenging fundamental Puritan beliefs. In the Colony, the church played a formal role in government; Williams sought to separate the two. In this early document, he explains that the "liberty of conscience" needed to be guaranteed by keeping the church out of the role of civil law. Modern readers may be struck by how much more theologically driven Williams's argument is than more recent secular defenses of religious freedom, including those in this volume. Williams's ideas in this text proved influential in later American thinking on religious freedom.

First, that the blood of so many hundred thousand souls of Protestants and Papists, spilt in the wars of present and former ages, for their respective consciences, is not required nor accepted by Jesus Christ the Prince of Peace.

Secondly, pregnant scriptures and arguments are throughout the work proposed against the doctrine of persecution for cause of conscience.

Thirdly, satisfactory answers are given to scriptures, and objections produced by Mr. Calvin, Beza, Mr. Cotton, and the ministers of the New English churches and others former and later, tending to prove the doctrine of persecution for cause of conscience.

Fourthly, the doctrine of persecution for cause of conscience is proved guilty of all the blood of the souls crying for vengeance under the altar.

Fifthly, all civil states with their officers of justice in their respective constitutions and administrations are proved essentially civil, and therefore not judges, governors, or defenders of the spiritual or Christian state and worship.

Sixthly, it is the will and command of God that (since the coming of his Son the Lord Jesus) a permission of the most paganish, Jewish, Turkish, or antichristian consciences and worships, be granted to all men in all nations and countries; and they are only to be fought against with that sword which is only (in soul matters) able to conquer, to wit, the sword of God's Spirit, the Word of God.

Seventhly, the state of the Land of Israel, the kings and people thereof in peace and war, is proved figurative and ceremonial, and no pattern nor president for any kingdom or civil state in the world to follow.

Eighthly, God requireth not a uniformity of religion to be enacted and enforced in any civil state; which enforced uniformity (sooner or later) is the greatest occasion of civil war, ravishing of conscience, persecution of Christ Jesus in his servants, and of the hypocrisy and destruction of millions of souls.

Ninthly, in holding an enforced uniformity of religion in a civil state, we must necessarily disclaim our desires and hopes of the Jew's conversion to Christ.

Tenthly, an enforced uniformity of religion throughout a

nation or civil state, confounds the civil and religious, denies the principles of Christianity and civility, and that Jesus Christ is come in the flesh.

Eleventhly, the permission of other consciences and worships than a state professeth only can (according to God) procure a firm and lasting peace (good assurance being taken according to the wisdom of the civil state for uniformity of civil obedience from all forts).

Twelfthly, lastly, true civility and Christianity may both flourish in a state or kingdom, notwithstanding the permission of divers and contrary consciences, either of Jew or Gentile. . . .

I acknowledge that to molest any person, Jew or Gentile, for either professing doctrine, or practicing worship merely religious or spiritual, it is to persecute him, and such a person (whatever his doctrine or practice be, true or false) suffereth persecution for conscience.

But withal I desire it may be well observed that this distinction is not full and complete: for beside this that a man may be persecuted because he holds or practices what he believes in conscience to be a truth (as Daniel did, for which he was cast into the lions' den, Dan. 6), and many thousands of Christians, because they durst not cease to preach and practice what they believed was by God commanded, as the Apostles answered (Acts 4 & 5), I say besides this a man may also be persecuted, because he dares not be constrained to yield obedience to such doctrines and worships as are by men invented and appointed. . . .

Dear Truth, I have two sad complaints:

First, the most sober of the witnesses, that dare to plead thy cause, how are they charged to be mine enemies, contentious, turbulent, seditious?

Secondly, thine enemies, though they speak and rail

against thee, though they outrageously pursue, imprison, banish, kill thy faithful witnesses, yet how is all vermilion'd o'er for justice against the heretics? Yea, if they kindle coals, and blow the flames of devouring wars, that leave neither spiritual nor civil state, but burn up branch and root, yet how do all pretend an holy war? He that kills, and he that's killed, they both cry out: "It is for God, and for their conscience."

'Tis true, nor one nor other seldom dare to plead the mighty Prince Christ Jesus for their author, yet (both Protestant and Papist) pretend they have spoke with Moses and the Prophets who all, say they (before Christ came), allowed such holy persecutions, holy wars against the enemies of holy church.

Truth (to ease thy first complaint), 'tis true, thy dearest sons, most like their mother, peacekeeping, peacemaking sons of God, have borne and still must bear the blurs of troublers of Israel, and turners of the world upside down. And 'tis true again, what Solomon once spake: "The beginning of strife is as when one letteth out water, therefore (saith he) leave off contention before it be meddled with. This caveat should keep the banks and sluices firm and strong, that strife, like a breach of waters, break not in upon the sons of men."

Yet strife must be distinguished: It is necessary or unnecessary, godly or Ungodly, Christian or unchristian, etc.

It is unnecessary, unlawful, dishonorable, ungodly, unchristian, in most cases in the world, for there is a possibility of keeping sweet peace in most cases, and, if it be possible, it is the express command of God that peace be kept (Rom. 13).

Again, it is necessary, honorable, godly, etc., with civil and earthly weapons to defend the innocent and to rescue the oppressed from the violent paws and jaws of oppressing persecuting Nimrods (Psal. 73; Job 29).

It is as necessary, yea more honorable, godly, and Christian, to fight the fight of faith, with religious and spiritual artillery, and to contend earnestly for the faith of Jesus, once delivered to the saints against all opposers, and the gates of earth and hell, men or devils, yea against Paul himself, or an angel from heaven, if he bring any other faith or doctrine. . . .

PEACE. I add that a civil sword (as woeful experience in all ages has proved) is so far from bringing or helping forward an opposite in religion to repentance that magistrates sin grievously against the work of God and blood of souls by such proceedings. Because as (commonly) the sufferings of false and antichristian teachers harden their followers, who being blind, by this means are occasioned to tumble into the ditch of hell after their blind leaders, with more inflamed zeal of lying confidence. So, secondly, violence and a sword of steel begets such an impression in the sufferers that certainly they conclude (as indeed that religion cannot be true which needs such instruments of violence to uphold it so) that persecutors are far from soft and gentle commiseration of the blindness of others. . . .

For (to keep to the similitude which the Spirit useth, for instance) to batter down a stronghold, high wall, fort, tower, or castle, men bring not a first and second admonition, and after obstinacy, excommunication, which are spiritual weapons concerning them that be in the church: nor exhortation to repent and be baptized, to believe in the Lord Jesus, etc., which are proper weapons to them that be without, etc. But to take a stronghold, men bring cannons, culverins, saker, bullets, powder, muskets, swords, pikes, etc., and these to this end are weapons effectual and proportionable.

On the other side, to batter down idolatry, false worship, heresy, schism, blindness, hardness, out of the soul and spirit, it is vain, improper, and unsuitable to bring those weapons which are used by persecutors, stocks, whips, prisons, swords, gibbets, stakes, etc. (where these seem to prevail with some cities or kingdoms, a stronger force sets up again, what a weaker pull'd down), but against these spiritual strongholds in the souls of men, spiritual artillery and weapons are proper, which are mighty through God to subdue and bring under the very thought to obedience, or else to bind fast the soul with chains of darkness, and lock it up in the prison of unbelief and hardness to eternity. . . .

Peace. I pray descend now to the second evil which you observe in the answerer's position that it would be evil to tolerate notorious evildoers, seducing teachers, etc.

TRUTH. I say the evil is that he most improperly and confusedly joins and couples seducing teachers with scandalous livers.

PEACE. But is it not true that the world is full of seducing teachers, and is it not true that seducing teachers are notorious evildoers?

TRUTH. I answer, far be it from me to deny either, and yet in two things I shall discover the great evil of this joining and coupling seducing teachers, and scandalous livers as one adequate or proper object of the magistrate's care and work to suppress and punish.

First, it is not an homogeneal (as we speak) but an hetergeneal commixture or joining together of things most different in kinds and natures, as if they were both of one consideration. . . .

I answer, in granting . . . that man hath not power to make laws to bind conscience, he overthrows such his tenet and practice as restrain men from their worship, according to their conscience and belief, and constrain them to such worships (though it be out of a pretense that they are convinced) which their own souls tell them they have no satisfaction nor faith in.

Secondly, whereas he affirms that men may make laws to see the laws of God observed.

I answer, God needeth not the help of a material sword of steel to assist the sword of the Spirit in the affairs of conscience, to those men, those magistrates, yea that commonwealth which makes such magistrates, must needs have power and authority from Christ Jesus to fit judge and to determine in all the great controversies concerning doctrine, discipline, government, etc.

And then I ask whether upon this ground it must not evidently follow that:

Either there is no lawful commonweal nor civil state of men in the world, which is not qualified with this spiritual discerning (and then also that the very commonweal hath more light concerning the church of Christ than the church itself).

Or, that the commonweal and magistrates thereof must judge and punish as they are persuaded in their own belief and conscience (be their conscience paganish, Turkish, or antichristian) what is this but to confound heaven and earth together, and not only to take away the being of Christianity out of the world, but to take away all civility, and the world out of the world, and to lay all upon heaps of confusion? . . .

The fourth head is the proper means of both these powers to attain their ends.

First, the proper means whereby the civil power may and should attain its end are only political, and principally these five.

First, the erecting and establishing what form of civil government may seem in wisdom most meet, according to general rules of the world, and state of the people.

Secondly, the making, publishing, and establishing of wholesome civil laws, not only such as concern civil justice, but also the free passage of true religion; for outward civil peace ariseth and is maintained from them both, from the latter as well as from the former.

Civil peace cannot stand entire, where religion is corrupted. . . . And yet such laws, though conversant about religion, may still be counted civil laws, as, on the contrary, an oath cloth still remain religious though conversant about civil matters.

Thirdly, election and appointment of civil officers to see execution to those laws.

Fourthly, civil punishments and rewards of transgressors and observers of these laws.

Fifthly, taking up arms against the enemies of civil peace.

Secondly, the means whereby the church may and should attain her ends are only ecclesiastical, which are chiefly five.

First, setting up that form of church government only of which Christ hath given them a pattern in his Word.

Secondly, acknowledging and admitting of no lawgiver in the church but Christ and the publishing of His laws.

Thirdly, electing and ordaining of such officers only, as Christ hath appointed in his Word.

Fourthly, to receive into their fellowship them that are approved and inflicting spiritual censures against them to that end.

Fifthly, prayer and patience in suffering any evil from them that be without, who disturb their peace.

So that magistrates, as magistrates, have no power of setting up the form of church government, electing church officers, punishing with church censures, but to see that the church does her duty herein. And on the other side, the churches as churches, have no power (though as members of the commonweal they may have power) of erecting or altering forms of civil government, electing of civil officers, inflicting civil punishments (no not on persons excommunicate) as by deposing magistrates from their civil authority, or withdrawing the hearts of the people against them, to their laws, no more than to discharge wives, or children, or servants, from due obedience to their husbands, parents, or masters; or by taking up arms against their magistrates, though he persecute them for conscience: for though members of churches who are public officers also of the civil state may suppress by force the violence of usurpers, as Iehoiada did Athaliah, yet this they do not as members of the church but as officers of the civil state.

Here are diverse considerable passages which I shall briefly examine, so far as concerns our controversy.

First, whereas they say that the civil power may erect and establish what form of civil government may seem in wisdom most meet, I acknowledge the proposition to be most true, both in itself and also considered with the end of it, that a civil government is an ordinance of God, to conserve the civil peace of people, so far as concerns their bodies and goods, as formerly hath been said.

But from this grant I infer (as before hath been touched) that the sovereign, original, and foundation of civil power lies in the people (whom they must needs mean by the civil power distinct from the government set up). And, if so, that a people may erect and establish what form of government seems to them most meet for their civil condition; it is evident that such governments as are by them erected and established have no more power, nor for no longer time, than the civil power or people consenting and agreeing shall betrust them with. This is clear not only in reason but in the experience of all commonweals, where the people are not deprived of their natural freedom by the power of tyrants.

And, if so, that the magistrates receive their power of

governing the church from the people, undeniably it follows that a people, as a people, naturally consider (of what nature or nation soever in Europe, Asia, Africa, or America), have fundamentally and originally, as men, a power to govern the church, to see her do her duty, to correct her, to redress, reform, establish, etc. And if this be not to pull God and Christ and Spirit out of heaven, and subject them unto natural, sinful, inconstant men, and so consequently to Satan himself, by whom all peoples naturally are guided, let heaven and earth judge. . . .

Some will here ask: What may the magistrate then lawfully do with his civil horn or power in matters of religion?

His horn not being the horn of that unicorn or rhinoceros, the power of the Lord Jesus in spiritual cases, his sword not the two-edged sword of the spirit, the word of God (hanging not about the loins or side, but at the lips. and proceeding out of the mouth of his ministers) but of an humane and civil nature and constitution, it must consequently be of a humane and civil operation, for who knows not that operation follows constitution; And therefore I shall end this passage with this consideration:

The civil magistrate either respecteth that religion and worship which his conscience is persuaded is true, and upon which he ventures his soul; or else that and those which he is persuaded are false.

Concerning the first, if that which the magistrate believeth to be true, be true, I say he owes a threefold duty unto it:

First, approbation and countenance, a reverent esteem and honorable testimony . . . with a tender respect of truth, and the professors of it.

Secondly, personal submission of his own soul to the

power of the Lord Jesus in that spiritual government and kingdom. . . .

Thirdly, protection of such true professors of Christ, whether apart, or met together, as also of their estates from violence and injury. . . .

Now, secondly, if it be a false religion (unto which the civil magistrate dare not adjoin, yet) he owes:

First, permission (for approbation he owes not what is evil) and this according to Matthew 13. 30 for public peace and quiet's sake.

Secondly, he owes protection to the persons of his subjects (though of a false worship), that no injury be offered either to the persons or goods of any. . . .

. . . The God of Peace, the God of Truth will shortly seal this truth, and confirm this witness, and make it evident to the whole world, that the doctrine of persecution for cause of conscience, is most evidently and lamentably contrary to the doctrine of Christ Jesus the Prince of Peace. Amen.

"A Letter Concerning Toleration," by *John Locke* (1689)

Along with Roger Williams's plea, another text that influenced the framers' views on religious freedom was John Locke's "A Letter Concerning Toleration." Locke is one of history's most important thinkers, an English philosopher whose views significantly shaped Revolutionary era political thought, including on religious freedom. In this letter, Locke does cite some biblical text, though he primarily advances a secular argument for religious toleration. As Locke argues, to provide for the liberty of conscience, government must ensure that secular reason, not one religious sect, governs civil society. Most obviously, that means dispensing with theocracy. Locke uses the example of the city of Constantinople to show that when two churches seek to impose their will on nonbelievers, the result is a lack of stability. Inevitably, a suppressed church will rebel from a governing church, leading to cycles of conflict that prohibit the flourishing of religion. To stop such a scenario, secular reasoning must predominate in the way government is organized and in how individual laws are made. That application of secular reasoning to lawmaking continues to influence our

> *own law of religion, notably in the Supreme Court's re-*
> *quirement that laws have a "secular" purpose.*

Honoured Sir,

Since you are pleased to inquire what are my Thoughts about the mutual Toleration of Christians in their different Professions of Religion, I must needs answer you freely, That I esteem that Toleration to be the chief Characteristical Mark of the True Church. For whatsoever some People boast of the Antiquity of Places and Names, or of the Pomp of their Outward Worship; Others, of the Reformation of their Discipline; All, of the Orthodoxy of their Faith; (for every one is Orthodox to himself): these things, and all others of this nature, are much rather Marks of Men striving for Power and Empire over one another, than of the Church of Christ. Let any one have never so true a Claim to all these things, yet if he be destitute of Charity, Meekness, and Good-will in general towards all Mankind; even to those that are not Christians, he is certainly yet short of being a true Christian himself. . . . Whosoever will list himself under the Banner of Christ, must in the first place, and above all things, make War upon his own Lusts and Vices. It is in vain for any Man to usurp the Name of Christian, without Holiness of Life, Purity of Manners, and Benignity and Meekness of Spirit.

. . . It would indeed be very hard for one that appears careless about his own Salvation, to perswade me that he were extreamly concern'd for mine. For it is impossible that those should sincerely and heartily apply themselves to make other People Christians, who have not really embraced the Christian Religion in their own Hearts. If the Gospel and the Apostles may be credited, no Man can be a Christian without *Charity*, and without *that Faith which works*, not by Force, but by *Love*. . . .

That any Man should think fit to cause another Man, whose Salvation he heartily desires, to expire in Torments, and that even in an unconverted estate; would, I confess, seem very strange to me; and, I think, to any other also. But no body, surely, will ever believe that such a Carriage can proceed from Charity, Love, or Good-will. If any one maintain that Men ought to be compelled by Fire and Sword to profess certain Doctrines, and conform to this or that exteriour Worship, without any regard had unto their Morals; if any one endeavour to convert those that are Erroneous unto the Faith, by forcing them to profess things that they do not believe, and allowing them to practise things that the Gospel does not permit; it cannot be doubted indeed but such a one is desirous to have a numerous Assembly joyned in the same Profession with himself. . . . If, like the Captain of our Salvation, they sincerely desired the Good of Souls, they would tread in the Steps, and follow the perfect Example of that Prince of Peace; who sent out his Soldiers to the subduing of Nations, and gathering them into his Church, not armed with the Sword, or other Instruments of Force, but prepared with the Gospel of Peace, and with the Exemplary Holiness of their Conversation. This was his Method. . . .

The Toleration of those that differ from others in Matters of Religion, is so agreeable to the Gospel of Jesus Christ, and to the genuine Reason of Mankind, that it seems monstrous for Men to be so blind, as not to perceive the Necessity and Advantage of it, in so clear a Light. . . .

The Commonwealth seems to me to be a Society of Men constituted only for the procuring, preserving, and advancing of their own *Civil Interests*.

Civil Interests I call Life, Liberty, Health, and Indolency of Body; and the Possession of outward things, such as Money, Lands, Houses, Furniture, and the like.

It is the Duty of the Civil Magistrate, by the impartial Execution of equal Laws, to secure unto all the People in general, and to every one of his Subjects in particular, the just Possession of these things belonging to this Life. . . .

Now that the whole Jurisdiction of the Magistrate reaches only to these civil Concernments; and that all Civil Power, Right, and Dominion, is bounded and confined to the only care of promoting these things; and that it neither can nor ought in any manner to be extended to the Salvation of Souls; these following Considerations seem unto me abundantly to demonstrate.

First, Because the Care of Souls is not committed to the Civil Magistrate any more than to other Men. It is not committed unto him, I say, by God; because it appears not that God has ever given any such Authority to one Man over another, as to compell any one to his Religion. Nor can any such Power be vested in the Magistrate by the *Consent of the People*; because no man can so far abandon the care of his own Salvation, as blindly to leave it to the choice of any other, whether Prince or Subject, to prescribe to him what Faith or Worship he shall embrace. For no Man can, if he would, conform his Faith to the Dictates, of another. All the Life and Power of true Religion consists in the inward and full perswasion of the mind: And Faith is not Faith without believing. Whatever Profession we make, to whatever outward Worship we conform, if we are not fully satisfied in our mind that the one is true, and the other well pleasing unto God; such Profession and such Practice, far from being any furtherance, are indeed great Obstacles to our Salvation. . . .

In the second place. The care of Souls cannot belong to the Civil Magistrate, because his Power consists only in outward

force: But true and saving Religion consists in the inward perswasion of the Mind; without which nothing can be acceptable
to God. And such is the nature of the Understanding, that it
cannot be compell'd to the belief of any thing by outward
Force. Confiscation of Estate, Imprisonment, Torments, nothing of that Nature can have any such Efficacy as to make Men
change the inward Judgment that they have framed of things.

It may indeed be alledged, that the Magistrate may make
use of Arguments, and thereby draw the Heterodox into the
way of Truth, and procure their Salvation. . . . But it is one
thing to perswade, another to command: One thing to press
with Arguments, another with Penalties. This the Civil Power
alone has a Right to do: to the other Good-will is Authority
enough. Every Man has Commission to admonish, exhort,
convince another of Error; and by reasoning to draw him into
Truth. But to give Laws, receive Obedience, and compel with
the Sword, belongs to none but the Magistrate. And upon this
ground I affirm, that the Magistrate's Power extends not to
the establishing of any Articles of Faith, or Forms of Worship,
by the force of his Laws. For Laws are of no force at all without Penalties, and Penalties in this case are absolutely imper-
tinent; because they are not proper to convince the mind. . . .
It is only Light and Evidence that can work a change in Mens
Opinions. And that Light can in no manner proceed from
corporal Sufferings, or any other outward Penalties. . . .

These Considerations, to omit many others that might have
been urged to the same purpose, seem unto me sufficient to
conclude that all the Power of Civil Government relates only
to Mens Civil Interests; is confined to the care of the things of
this World; and hath nothing to do with the World to come.

Let us now consider what a Church is. A Church then I take
to be a voluntary Society of Men, joining themselves together
of their own accord, in order to the publick worshipping of

God, in such a manner as they judge acceptable to him, and effectual to the Salvation of their Souls.

I say it is a free and voluntary Society. No body is born a Member of any Church. Otherwise the Religion of Parents would descend unto Children, by the same right of Inheritance as their Temporal Estates, and every one would hold his Faith by the same Tenure he does his Lands; than which nothing can be imagined more absurd. Thus therefore that matter stands. No Man by nature is bound unto any particular Church or Sect, but every one joins himself voluntarily to that Society in which he believes he has found that Profession and Worship which is truly acceptable unto God. The hopes of Salvation, as it was the only cause of his entrance into that Communion, so it can be the only reason of his stay there. For if afterwards he discover any thing either erroneous in the Doctrine, or incongruous in the Worship of that Society to which he has join'd himself; Why should it not be as free for him to go out, as it was to enter? No Member of a Religious Society can be tied with any other Bonds but what proceed from the certain expectation of eternal Life. A Church then is a Society of Members voluntarily uniting to this end. . . .

These things being thus determined, let us inquire in the next place, how far the Duty of Toleration extends; and what is required from every one by it.

And first, I hold, That no Church is bound by the Duty of Toleration to retain any such Person in her Bosom, as, after Admonition, continues obstinately to offend against the Laws of the Society. For these being the Condition of Communion, and the Bond of the Society; If the Breach of them were permitted without any Animadversion, the Society would immediately be thereby dissolved. But nevertheless, in all such Cases, care is to be taken that the Sentence of Excommunication, and the Execution thereof, carry with it no rough usage of Word or Action, whereby the ejected Person may any wise be damnified in Body or Estate. For all Force (as has often been said) belongs only to the Magistrate; nor ought any private Persons, at any time, to use Force, unless it be in Self-defence against unjust Violence. Excommunication neither does, nor can deprive the excommunicated Person of any of those Civil Goods that he formerly possessed. All those things belong to the Civil Government, and are under the Magistrate's Protection. The whole Force of Excommunication consists only in this, that the Resolution of the Society in that respect being declared, the Union that was between the Body and some Member comes thereby to be dissolved; and that Relation ceasing; the participation of some certain things, which the Society communicated to its Members, and unto which no Man has any Civil Right, comes also to cease. . . .

Secondly, No private Person has any Right, in any manner, to prejudice another Person in his Civil Enjoyments, because he is of another Church or Religion. All the Rights and Franchises that belong to him as a Man . . . are inviolably to be Preserved to him. These are not the Business of Religion. No Violence nor Injury is to be offered him, whether he be Christian or Pagan. Nay, we must not content our selves with the narrow Measures of bare Justice. Charity, Bounty, and Liberality must be added to it. This the Gospel enjoyns; this Reason directs; and this that natural Fellowship we are born into requires of us. If any man err from the right way, it is his own Misfortune, no Injury to thee: Nor therefore art thou to punish him in the things of this Life, because thou supposest he will be miserable in that which is to come.

What I say concerning the mutual Toleration of private Persons differing from one another in Religion, I understand also of particular Churches; which stand as it were in the same relation to each other as private Persons among themselves;

nor has any one of them any manner of Jurisdiction over any other, no not even when the Civil Magistrate (as it sometimes happens) comes to be of this or the other Communion. . . .

That the thing may be made yet clearer by an Example; Let us suppose two Churches, the one of *Arminians*, the other of *Calvinists*, residing in the City of *Constantinople*; Will any one say, that either of these Churches has Right to deprive the Members of the other of their Estates and Liberty, (as we see practised elsewhere) because of their differing from it in some Doctrines or Ceremonies; whilst the *Turks* in the mean while silently stand by, and laugh to see with what inhumane Cruelty Christians thus rage against Christians? But if one of these Churches hath this Power of treating the other ill, I ask which of them it is to whom that Power belongs, and by what Right? It will be answered undoubtedly, That it is the Orthodox Church which has the Right of Authority over the Erroneous or Heretical. This is, in great and specious words, to say just nothing at all. For every Church is Orthodox to it self; to others, Erroneous or Heretical. Whatsoever any Church believes, it believes to be true; and the contrary thereunto it pronounces to be Error. So that the Controversie between these Churches about the Truth of their Doctrines, and the Purity of their Worship, is on both sides equal; nor is there any Judge, either at *Constantinople*, or elsewhere upon Earth, by whose Sentence it can be determined. The Decision of that Question belongs only to the Supream Judge of all men, to whom also alone belongs the Punishment of the Erroneous. In the mean while, let those men consider how hainously they sin; Who, adding Injustice, if not to their Error, yet certainly to their Pride, do rashly and arrogantly take upon them to misuse the Servants of another Master, who are not at all accountable to them.

Nay further: If it could be manifest which of these two

dissenting Churches were in the right way, there would not accrue thereby to the Orthodox any Right of destroying the other. For Churches have neither any Jurisdiction in worldly Matters, nor are Fire and Sword any proper Instruments wherewith to convince mens Minds of Error, and inform them of the Truth. Let us suppose, nevertheless, that the Civil Magistrate inclined to favour one of them, and to put his Sword into their Hands; that (by his consent) they might chastise the Dissenters as they pleased. Will any man say, that any Right can be derived unto a Christian Church over its Brethren, from a Turkish Emperor? An Infidel, who has himself no Authority to punish Christians for the Articles of their Faith, cannot confer such an Authority upon any Society of Christians, nor give unto them a Right, which he has not himself. This would be the Case at *Constantinople*. And the Reason of the thing is the same in any Christian Kingdom. The Civil Power is the same in every place; nor can that Power, in the Hands of a Christian Prince, confer any greater Authority upon the Church, than in the Hands of a Heathen; which is to say, just none at all. . . .

No body . . . neither single Persons, nor Churches, nay, nor even Commonwealths, have any just Title to invade the Civil Rights and Worldly Goods of each other upon pretence of Religion. Those that are of another Opinion, would do well to consider with themselves how pernicious a Seed of Discord and War, how powerful a Provocation to endless Hatreds, Rapines, and Slaughters, they thereby furnish unto Mankind. No Peace and Security, no not so much as common Friendship, can ever be established or preserved amongst Men, so long as this Opinion prevails, That *Dominion is founded in Grace*, and that Religion is to be propagated by force of Arms.

In the third Place, Let us see what the *Duty of Toleration* requires from those who are distinguished from the rest of

Mankind . . . by some *Ecclesiastical Character and Office*; whether they be Bishops, Priests, Presbyters, Ministers, or however else dignified or distinguished. It is not my Business to enquire here into the Original of the Power or Dignity of the Clergy. This only I say, That whence-soever their Authority be sprung, since it is Ecclesiastical, it ought to be confined within the Bounds of the Church, nor can it in any manner be extended to Civil Affairs; because the Church it self is a thing absolutely separate and distinct from the Commonwealth. . . . No man therefore, with whatsoever Ecclesiastical Office he be dignified, can deprive another man, that is not of his Church and Faith, either of Liberty, or of any part of his Worldly Goods, upon the account of that difference which is between them in Religion. . . .

But this is not all. It is not enough that Ecclesiastical Men abstain from Violence and Rapine, and all manner of Persecution. He that pretends to be a Successor of the Apostles, and takes upon him the Office of Teaching, is obliged also to admonish his Hearers of the Duties of Peace and Good-will towards all men; as well towards the Erroneous, as the Orthodox; towards those that differ from them in Faith and Worship, as well as towards those that agree with them therein. . . .

. . . Let us now consider *what is the Magistrate's Duty* in the Business of Toleration; which certainly is very considerable. . . .

. . . The *Principal Consideration*, and which absolutely determines this Controversie, is this. Although the Magistrates Opinion in Religion be sound, and the way that he appoints be truly Evangelical, yet if I be not thoroughly perswaded thereof in my own mind, there will be no safety for me in following it. No way whatsoever that I shall walk in, against the Dictates of my Conscience, will ever bring me to the Mansions of the Blessed. I may grow rich by an Art that I take not delight in; I may be cured of some Disease by Remedies that I have not Faith in; but I cannot be saved by a Religion that I distrust, and by a Worship that I abhor. It is in vain for an Unbeliever to take up the outward shew of another Mans Profession. Faith only, and inward Sincerity, are the things that procure acceptance with God. The most likely and most approved Remedy can have no effect upon the Patient, if his Stomach reject it as soon as taken. And you will in vain cram a Medicine down a sick Mans Throat, which his particular Constitution will be sure to turn into Poison. In a word. Whatsoever may be doubtful in Religion, yet this at least is certain, that no Religion, which I believe not to be true, can be either true or profitable unto me. In vain therefore do Princes compel their Subjects to come into their Church-communion, under pretence of saving their Souls. If they believe, they will come of their own accord; if they believe not, their coming will nothing avail them. How great soever, in fine, may be the pretence of Good-will and Charity, and concern for the Salvation of Mens Souls; Men cannot be forced to be saved whether they will or no. And therefore, when all is done, they must be left to their own Consciences. . . .

These Religious Societies I call Churches: and these I say the Magistrate ought to tolerate. For the business of these Assemblies of the People is nothing but what is lawful for every Man in particular to take care of; I mean the Salvation of their Souls. Nor in this case is there any difference between the National Church, and other separated Congregations.

But as in every Church there are two things especially to be considered; *The outward Form and Rites of Worship; And the Doctrines and Articles of Faith*; These things must be handled each distinctly; that so the whole matter of Toleration may the more clearly be understood.

Concerning outward Worship, I say . . . that the Magistrate has no Power to enforce by Law, either in his own Church, or much less in another, the use of any Rites or Ceremonies whatsoever in the Worship of God. And this, not only because these Churches are free Societies; but because whatsoever is practiced in the Worship of God, is only so far justifiable as it is believed by those that practise it to be acceptable unto him. Whatsoever is not done with that Assurance of Faith, is neither well in it self, nor can it be acceptable to God. To impose such things therefore upon any People, contrary to their own Judgment, is in effect to command them to offend God; Which, considering that the end of all Religion is to please him, and that Liberty is essentially necessary to that End, appears to be absurd beyond expression. . . .

In the next place: As the Magistrate has no Power to *impose* by his Laws, the use of any Rites and Ceremonies in any Church; so neither has he any Power to *forbid* the use of such Rites and Ceremonies as are already received, approved, and practised by any Church. Because if he did so, he would destroy the Church it self; the end of whose Institution is only to worship God with freedom, after its own manner.

You will say, by this Rule, if some Congregations should have a mind to *sacrifice Infants*, or (as the Primitive Christians were falsly accused) *lustfully pollute themselves in promiscuous Uncleanness*, or practise any other such heinous Enormities, *is the Magistrate obliged to tolerate them*, because they are committed in a Religious Assembly? I answer, No. These things are not lawful in the ordinary course of life, nor in any private house; and therefore neither are they so in the Worship of God, or in any Religious Meeting. But indeed if any People congregated upon account of Religion, should be desirous to sacrifice a Calf, I deny that That ought to be prohibited by a Law. . . .

By this we see what difference there is between the Church

and the Common-wealth. Whatsoever is lawful in the Common-wealth, cannot be prohibited by the Magistrate in the Church. Whatsoever is permitted unto any one of his Subjects for their ordinary use, neither can, nor ought to be forbidden by him to any Sect of People for their Religious Uses. If any man may lawfully take Bread or Wine, either sitting or kneeling, in his own house, the Law ought not to abridge him of the same Liberty in his Religious Worship; though in the Church the use of Bread and Wine be very different, and be there applied to the Mysteries of Faith, and Rites of Divine Worship. But those things that are prejudicial to the Common weal of a People in their ordinary use, and are therefore forbidden by Laws, those things ought not to be permitted to Churches in their Sacred Rites. Only the Magistrate ought always to be very careful, that he do not misuse his Authority, to the oppression of any Church, under pretence of publick Good. . . .

Further, The Magistrate ought not to forbid the Preaching or Professing of any Speculative Opinions in any Church; because they have no manner of relation to the Civil Rights of the Subjects. If a *Roman Catho-lick* believe that to be really the Body of Christ, which another man calls Bread, he does no injury thereby to his Neighbour. If a *Jew* do not believe the New Testament to be the Word of God, he does not thereby alter any thing in mens Civil Rights. If a Heathen doubt of both Testaments, he is not therefore to be punished as a pernicious Citizen. The Power of the Magistrate, and the Estates of the People, may be equally secure, whether any man believe these things or no. I readily grant, that these Opinions are false and absurd. But the business of Laws is not to provide for the Truth of Opinions, but for the Safety and Security of the Commonwealth, and of every particular mans Goods and Person. And so it ought to be. . . .

. . . The *Sum of all* we drive at is, *That every Man may enjoy the same Rights that are granted to others.* . . . Whatsoever things are left free by Law in the common occasions of Life, let them remain free unto every Church in Divine Worship. Let no Mans Life, or Body, or House, or Estate, suffer any manner of Prejudice upon these Accounts. . . .

. . . [T]hose whose Doctrine is peaceable, and whose Manners are pure and blameless, ought to be upon equal Terms with their Fellow Subjects. Thus if Solemn Assemblies, Observations of Festivals, Publick Worship, be permitted to any one sort of Professors; all these things ought to be permitted to the *Presbyterians*, *Independents*, *Anabaptists*, *Arminians*, *Quakers*, and others, with the same liberty. Nay if we may openly speak the Truth and as becomes one Man to another; neither *Pagan*, nor *Mahumetan*, nor *Jew*, ought to be excluded from the Civil Rights of the Commonwealth, because of his Religion. . . .

. . . God Almighty grant, I beseech him, that the Gospel of Peace may at length be Preached, and that Civil Magistrates growing more careful to conform their own Consciences to the Law of God, and less solicitous about the binding of other mens Consciences by Humane Laws, may, like Fathers of their Countrey, direct all their Counsels and Endeavours to promote universally the Civil Welfare of all their Children; except only of such as are arrogant, ungovernable, and injurious to their Brethren; and that all Ecclesiastical men, who boast themselves to be the Successors of the Apostles, walking peaceably and modestly in the Apostles steps, without intermedling with State-Affairs, may apply themselves wholly to promote the Salvation of Souls.

Farewel.

"Memorial and Remonstrance against Religious Assessments," by *James Madison* (1785)

The occasion for this piece by James Madison, written two years before the Constitutional Convention, was a proposal in the Virginia legislature that would have established a "provision for the teachers of the Christian religion." The legislation would have given money directly to churches to fund ministers and other religious teachers. Although the bill would not establish a formal theocracy, Madison's language makes it clear he saw this bill as more than just standard education funding. In fact, he warns that in the past, the mixing of religion and government has led to "tyranny." Madison's arguments echo Locke's in objecting to religious reasons inflecting secular lawmaking. Madison argues forcefully that even a secular government cannot provide public funds for religious purposes without risking religious tyranny. His arguments also go beyond Locke's in many ways, as he posits that religious freedom requires not just the rejection of an official church, but the rejection of laws that improperly advantage certain religions over others. The piece remains crucial to understanding the intent of the Establishment Clause Madison would later draft banning laws "respecting," or related to, establishment of religion by government.

TO THE HONORABLE THE GENERAL ASSEMBLY OF THE COMMONWEALTH OF VIRGINIA

A Memorial and Remonstrance

We the subscribers, citizens of the said Commonwealth, having taken into serious consideration, a Bill printed by order of the last Session of General Assembly, entitled "A Bill establishing a provision for Teachers of the Christian Religion," and conceiving that the same if finally armed with the sanctions of a law, will be a dangerous abuse of power, are bound as faithful members of a free State to remonstrate against it, and to declare the reasons by which we are determined. We remonstrate against the said Bill,

1. Because we hold it for a fundamental and undeniable truth, "that Religion or the duty which we owe to our Creator and the manner of discharging it, can be directed only by reason and conviction, not by force or violence." The Religion then of every man must be left to the conviction and conscience of every man; and it is the right of every man to exercise it as these may dictate. This right is in its nature an unalienable right. It is unalienable, because the opinions of men, depending only on the evidence contemplated by their own minds cannot follow the dictates of other men: It is unalienable also, because what is here a right towards men, is a duty towards the Creator. It is the duty of every man to render to the Creator such homage and such only as he believes to be acceptable to him. This duty is precedent, both in order of time and in degree of obligation, to the claims of Civil

Society. Before any man can be considered as a member of Civil Society, he must be considered as a subject of the Governour of the Universe: And if a member of Civil Society, who enters into any subordinate Association, must always do it with a reservation of his duty to the General Authority; much more must every man who becomes a member of any particular Civil Society, do it with a saving of his allegiance to the Universal Sovereign. We maintain therefore that in matters of Religion, no mans right is abridged by the institution of Civil Society and that Religion is wholly exempt from its cognizance. True it is, that no other rule exists, by which any question which may divide a Society, can be ultimately determined, but the will of the majority; but it is also true that the majority may trespass on the rights of the minority.

2. Because if Religion be exempt from the authority of the Society at large, still less can it be subject to that of the Legislative Body. The latter are but the creatures and vicegerents of the former. Their jurisdiction is both derivative and limited: it is limited with regard to the co-ordinate departments, more necessarily is it limited with regard to the constituents. The preservation of a free Government requires not merely, that the metes and bounds which separate each department of power be invariably maintained; but more especially that neither of them be suffered to overleap the great Barrier which defends the rights of the people. The Rulers who are guilty of such an encroachment, exceed the commission from which they derive their authority, and are Tyrants. The People who submit to it are governed by laws made neither by themselves nor by an authority derived from them, and are slaves.

3. Because it is proper to take alarm at the first experiment on our liberties. We hold this prudent jealousy to be the first duty of Citizens, and one of the noblest characteristics of the late Revolution. The free men of America did not wait till

usurped power had strengthened itself by exercise, and entangled the question in precedents. They saw all the consequences in the principle, and they avoided the consequences by denying the principle. We revere this lesson too much soon to forget it. Who does not see that the same authority which can establish Christianity, in exclusion of all other Religions, may establish with the same ease any particular sect of Christians, in exclusion of all other Sects? that the same authority which can force a citizen to contribute three pence only of his property for the support of any one establishment, may force him to conform to any other establishment in all cases whatsoever?

4. Because the Bill violates that equality which ought to be the basis of every law, and which is more indispensible, in proportion as the validity or expediency of any law is more liable to be impeached. If "all men are by nature equally free and independent," all men are to be considered as entering into Society on equal conditions; as relinquishing no more, and therefore retaining no less, one than another, of their natural rights. Above all are they to be considered as retaining an "equal title to the free exercise of Religion according to the dictates of Conscience." Whilst we assert for ourselves a freedom to embrace, to profess and to observe the Religion which we believe to be of divine origin, we cannot deny an equal freedom to those whose minds have not yet yielded to the evidence which has convinced us. If this freedom be abused, it is an offence against God, not against man: To God, therefore, not to man, must an account of it be rendered. As the Bill violates equality by subjecting some to peculiar burdens, so it violates the same principle, by granting to others peculiar exemptions. Are the Quakers and Menonists the only sects who think a compulsive support of their Religions unnecessary and unwarrantable? Can their piety alone be entrusted with the care of public worship? Ought their Religions to be endowed above all others with extraordinary privileges by which proselytes may be enticed from all others? We think too favorably of the justice and good sense of these denominations to believe that they either covet preeminences over their fellow citizens or that they will be seduced by them from the common opposition to the measure.

5. Because the Bill implies either that the Civil Magistrate is a competent Judge of Religious Truth; or that he may employ Religion as an engine of Civil policy. The first is an arrogant pretension falsified by the contradictory opinions of Rulers in all ages, and throughout the world: the second an unhallowed perversion of the means of salvation.

6. Because the establishment proposed by the Bill is not requisite for the support of the Christian Religion. To say that it is, is a contradiction to the Christian Religion itself, for every page of it disavows a dependence on the powers of this world: it is a contradiction to fact; for it is known that this Religion both existed and flourished, not only without the support of human laws, but in spite of every opposition from them, and not only during the period of miraculous aid, but long after it had been left to its own evidence and the ordinary care of Providence. Nay, it is a contradiction in terms; for a Religion not invented by human policy, must have preexisted and been supported, before it was established by human policy. It is moreover to weaken in those who profess this Religion a pious confidence in its innate excellence and the patronage of its Author; and to foster in those who still reject it, a suspicion that its friends are too conscious of its fallacies to trust it to its own merits.

7. Because experience witnesseth that ecclesiastical establishments, instead of maintaining the purity and efficacy of Religion, have had a contrary operation. During almost fifteen centuries has the legal establishment of Christianity been on trial. What have been its fruits? More or less in all places, pride and indolence in the Clergy, ignorance and servility in the laity, in both, superstition, bigotry and persecution. Enquire of the Teachers of Christianity for the ages in which it appeared in its greatest lustre; those of every sect, point to the ages prior to its incorporation with Civil policy. Propose a restoration of this primitive State in which its Teachers depended on the voluntary rewards of their flocks, many of them predict its downfall. On which Side ought their testimony to have greatest weight, when for or when against their interest?

8. Because the establishment in question is not necessary for the support of Civil Government. If it be urged as necessary for the support of Civil Government only as it is a means of supporting Religion, and it be not necessary for the latter purpose, it cannot be necessary for the former. If Religion be not within the cognizance of Civil Government how can its legal establishment be necessary to Civil Government? What influence in fact have ecclesiastical establishments had on Civil Society? In some instances they have been seen to erect a spiritual tyranny on the ruins of the Civil authority; in many instances they have been seen upholding the thrones of political tyranny: in no instance have they been seen the guardians of the liberties of the people. Rulers who wished to subvert the public liberty, may have found an established Clergy convenient auxiliaries. A just Government instituted to secure & perpetuate it needs them not. Such a Government will be best supported by protecting every Citizen in the enjoyment of his Religion with the same equal hand which protects his person and his property; by neither invading the equal rights of any Sect, nor suffering any Sect to invade those of another.

9. Because the proposed establishment is a departure from that generous policy, which, offering an Asylum to the persecuted and oppressed of every Nation and Religion, promised a lustre to our country, and an accession to the number of its citizens. What a melancholy mark is the Bill of sudden degeneracy? Instead of holding forth an Asylum to the persecuted, it is itself a signal of persecution. It degrades from the equal rank of Citizens all those whose opinions in Religion do not bend to those of the Legislative authority. Distant as it may be in its present form from the Inquisition, it differs from it only in degree. The one is the first step, the other the last in the career of intolerance. The magnanimous sufferer under this cruel scourge in foreign Regions, must view the Bill as a Beacon on our Coast, warning him to seek some other haven, where liberty and philanthropy in their due extent, may offer a more certain repose from his Troubles.

10. Because it will have a like tendency to banish our Citizens. The allurements presented by other situations are every day thinning their number. To superadd a fresh motive to emigration by revoking the liberty which they now enjoy, would be the same species of folly which has dishonoured and depopulated flourishing kingdoms.

11. Because it will destroy that moderation and harmony which the forbearance of our laws to intermeddle with Religion has produced among its several sects. Torrents of blood have been spilt in the old world, by vain attempts of the secular arm, to extinguish Religious discord, by proscribing all difference in Religious opinion. Time has at length revealed the true remedy. Every relaxation of narrow and rigorous policy, wherever it has been tried, has been found to assuage the disease. The American Theatre has exhibited proofs that equal and compleat liberty, if it does not wholly eradicate it, sufficiently destroys its malignant influence on the health and prosperity of the State. If with the salutary effects of this system under our own eyes, we begin to contract the bounds of Religious freedom, we know no name that will too severely reproach our folly. At least let warning be taken at the first fruits of the threatened innovation. The very appearance of the Bill has transformed "that Christian forbearance, love and charity," which of late mutually prevailed, into animosities and jealousies, which may not soon be appeased. What mischiefs may not be dreaded, should this enemy to the public quiet be armed with the force of a law?

12. Because the policy of the Bill is adverse to the diffusion of the light of Christianity. The first wish of those who enjoy this precious gift ought to be that it may be imparted to the whole race of mankind. Compare the number of those who have as yet received it with the number still remaining under the dominion of false Religions; and how small is the former! Does the policy of the Bill tend to lessen the disproportion? No; it at once discourages those who are strangers to the light of revelation from coming into the Region of it; and countenances by example the nations who continue in darkness, in shutting out those who might convey it to them. Instead of Levelling as far as possible, every obstacle to the victorious progress of Truth, the Bill with an ignoble and unchristian timidity would circumscribe it with a wall of defence against the encroachments of error.

13. Because attempts to enforce by legal sanctions, acts obnoxious to so great a proportion of Citizens, tend to enervate the laws in general, and to slacken the bands of Society. If it be difficult to execute any law which is not generally deemed necessary or salutary, what must be the case, where it is deemed invalid and dangerous? And what may be the effect of so striking an example of impotency in the Government, on its general authority?

14. Because a measure of such singular magnitude and delicacy ought not to be imposed, without the clearest evidence

that it is called for by a majority of citizens, and no satisfactory method is yet proposed by which the voice of the majority in this case may be determined, or its influence secured. "The people of the respective counties are indeed requested to signify their opinion respecting the adoption of the Bill to the next Session of Assembly." But the representation must be made equal, before the voice either of the Representatives or of the Counties will be that of the people. Our hope is that neither of the former will, after due consideration, espouse the dangerous principle of the Bill. Should the event disappoint us, it will still leave us in full confidence, that a fair appeal to the latter will reverse the sentence against our liberties. **15.** Because finally, "the equal right of every citizen to the free exercise of his Religion according to the dictates of conscience" is held by the same tenure with all our other rights. If we recur to its origin, it is equally the gift of nature; if we weigh its importance, it cannot be less dear to us; if we consult the "Declaration of those rights which pertain to the good people of Virginia, as the basis and foundation of Government," it is enumerated with equal solemnity, or rather studied emphasis. Either then, we must say, that the Will of the Legislature is the only measure of their authority; and that in the plenitude of this authority, they may sweep away all our fundamental rights; or, that they are bound to leave this particular right untouched and sacred: Either we must say, that they may controul the freedom of the press, may abolish the Trial by Jury, may swallow up the Executive and Judiciary Powers of the State; nay that they may despoil us of our very right of suffrage, and erect themselves into an independent and hereditary Assembly or, we must say, that they have no authority to enact into law the Bill under consideration. We the Subscribers say, that the General Assembly of this Commonwealth have no such authority: And that no effort may be omitted on our part against so dangerous an usurpation, we oppose to it, this remonstrance; earnestly praying, as we are in duty bound, that the Supreme Lawgiver of the Universe, by illuminating those to whom it is addressed, may on the one hand, turn their Councils from every act which would affront his holy prerogative, or violate the trust committed to them: and on the other, guide them into every measure which may be worthy of his [blessing, may re]dound to their own praise, and may establish more firmly the liberties, the prosperity and the happiness of the Commonwealth.

"The Virginia Statute for Religious Freedom," by *Thomas Jefferson* (1786)

Having defeated the bill to fund religious education, James Madison sought to codify the approach to religious freedom he favored. He supported a bill drafted by his ally and friend Thomas Jefferson outlining twin pillars of religious freedom. Notice here that Jefferson's bill guarantees the freedom to worship and places limits on government interference with religious practice. That is no accident for Jefferson, who, like Madison, believed that limiting the government's use of religious reasons—the principle that would later become enshrined in the Establishment Clause—is necessary to guarantee the freedom to worship as one wishes.

AN ACT FOR ESTABLISHING RELIGIOUS FREEDOM.

Whereas, Almighty God hath created the mind free;

That all attempts to influence it by temporal punishments or burthens, or by civil incapacitations tend only to beget habits of hypocrisy and meanness, and are a departure from the plan of the holy author of our religion, who being Lord, both of body and mind yet chose not to propagate it by coercions on either, as was in his Almighty power to do,

That the impious presumption of legislators and rulers, civil as well as ecclesiastical, who, being themselves but fallible and uninspired men have assumed dominion over the faith of others, setting up their own opinions and modes of thinking as the only true and infallible, and as such endeavouring to impose them on others, hath established and maintained false religions over the greatest part of the world and through all time;

That to compel a man to furnish contributions of money for the propagation of opinions which he disbelieves is sinful and tyrannical;

That even the forcing him to support this or that teacher of his own religious persuasion is depriving him of the comfortable liberty of giving his contributions to the particular pastor, whose morals he would make his pattern, and whose powers he feels most persuasive to righteousness, and is withdrawing from the Ministry those temporary rewards, which, proceeding from an approbation of their personal conduct are an additional incitement to earnest and unremitting labours for the instruction of mankind;

That our civil rights have no dependence on our religious opinions any more than our opinions in physics or geometry,

That therefore the proscribing any citizen as unworthy the public confidence, by laying upon him an incapacity of being called to offices of trust and emolument, unless he profess or renounce this or that religious opinion, is depriving him injuriously of those privileges and advantages, to which, in common with his fellow citizens, he has a natural right,

That it tends only to corrupt the principles of that very

Religion it is meant to encourage, by bribing with a monopoly of worldly honours and emoluments those who will externally profess and conform to it;

That though indeed, these are criminal who do not withstand such temptation, yet neither are those innocent who lay the bait in their way;

That to suffer the civil magistrate to intrude his powers into the field of opinion and to restrain the profession or propagation of principles on supposition of their ill tendency is a dangerous fallacy which at once destroys all religious liberty because he being of course judge of that tendency will make his opinions the rule of judgment and approve or condemn the sentiments of others only as they shall square with or differ from his own;

That it is time enough for the rightful purposes of civil government, for its officers to interfere when principles break out into overt acts against peace and good order;

And finally, that Truth is great, and will prevail if left to herself, that she is the proper and sufficient antagonist to error, and has nothing to fear from the conflict, unless by human interposition disarmed of her natural weapons free argument and debate, errors ceasing to be dangerous when it is permitted freely to contradict them:

Be it enacted by General Assembly that no man shall be compelled to frequent or support any religious worship, place, or ministry whatsoever, nor shall be enforced, restrained, molested, or burthened in his body or goods, nor shall otherwise suffer on account of his religious opinions or belief, but that all men shall be free to profess, and by argument to maintain, their opinions in matters of Religion, and that the same shall in no wise diminish, enlarge or affect their civil capacities. And though we well know that this Assembly elected by the people for the ordinary purposes of

Legislation only, have no power to restrain the acts of succeeding Assemblies constituted with powers equal to our own, and that therefore to declare this act irrevocable would be of no effect in law; yet we are free to declare, and do declare that the rights hereby asserted, are of the natural rights of mankind, and that if any act shall be hereafter passed to repeal the present or to narrow its operation, such act will be an infringement of natural right.

First Amendment to the *United States Constitution* (1791)

The First Amendment outlines two religion "clauses." The Establishment Clause places a ban on passing laws that would create an official church of the United States or otherwise establish an official government religion. The Free Exercise Clause guarantees that individuals have the freedom to practice their religion without government interference. Though short, both clauses have been the source of deep controversy and various interpretations of meaning.

AMENDMENT I

Congress shall make no law respecting an establishment of religion, or prohibiting the free exercise thereof; or abridging the freedom of speech, or of the press, or the right of the people peaceably to assemble, and to petition the Government for a redress of grievances.

Part II

CHURCH
and
STATE

"Letter to Touro Synagogue," by *George Washington* (1790)

Washington's letter—and his choice to visit the country's first synagogue—is an important early statement of religious freedom in the constitutional system. It makes clear that the young republic would do more than merely tolerate religious minorities, and instead, would protect their practice. Soon after Washington's letter, delivered strategically during the debate over ratification of the Bill of Rights, the First Amendment was ratified, guaranteeing the religious freedom that Washington championed through its Free Exercise and Establishment Clauses.

Gentlemen:

While I received with much satisfaction your address replete with expressions of esteem, I rejoice in the opportunity of assuring you that I shall always retain grateful remembrance of the cordial welcome I experienced on my visit to Newport from all classes of citizens.

The reflection on the days of difficulty and danger which are past is rendered the more sweet from a consciousness that they are succeeded by days of uncommon prosperity and security.

If we have wisdom to make the best use of the advantages with which we are now favored, we cannot fail, under the just administration of a good government, to become a great and happy people.

The citizens of the United States of America have a right to applaud themselves for having given to mankind examples of an enlarged and liberal policy—a policy worthy of imitation. All possess alike liberty of conscience and immunities of citizenship.

It is now no more that toleration is spoken of as if it were the indulgence of one class of people that another enjoyed the exercise of their inherent natural rights, for, happily, the Government of the United States, which gives to bigotry no sanction, to persecution no assistance, requires only that they who live under its protection should demean themselves as good citizens in giving it on all occasions their effectual support.

It would be inconsistent with the frankness of my character not to avow that I am pleased with your favorable opinion of my administration and fervent wishes for my felicity.

May the children of the stock of Abraham who dwell in this land continue to merit and enjoy the good will of the other inhabitants—while every one shall sit in safety under his own vine and fig tree and there shall be none to make him afraid.

May the father of all mercies scatter light, and not darkness, upon our paths, and make us all in our several vocations useful here, and in His own due time and way everlastingly happy.

G. Washington

"Letter to the Danbury Baptists," by *Thomas Jefferson* (1802)

This letter is famous for Jefferson's use of the phrase "wall of separation" to explain his view of the proper constitutional relationship between church and state. However, many scholars find that metaphor too strict. According to the Court's current interpretation of the First Amendment, government is banned from some intervention in church affairs, and there are strong limits on the role religious reasons can play in government decision making. However, as we will see, there are many cases in which the boundaries between the two spheres are complicated, with an impermeable "wall" impossible.

TO MESSERS. NEHEMIAH DODGE, EPHRAIM ROBBINS, & STEPHEN S. NELSON, A COMMITTEE OF THE DANBURY BAPTIST ASSOCIATION IN THE STATE OF CONNECTICUT.

Gentlemen

The affectionate sentiments of esteem and approbation which you are so good as to express towards me, on behalf of the Danbury Baptist association, give me the highest satisfaction. My duties dictate a faithful and zealous pursuit of the interests of my constituents, & in proportion as they are persuaded of my fidelity to those duties, the discharge of them becomes more and more pleasing.

Believing with you that religion is a matter which lies solely between Man & his God, that he owes account to none other for his faith or his worship, that the legitimate powers of government reach actions only, & not opinions, I contemplate with sovereign reverence that act of the whole American people which declared that their legislature should "make no law respecting an establishment of religion, or prohibiting the free exercise thereof," thus building a wall of separation between Church & State. Adhering to this expression of the supreme will of the nation in behalf of the rights of conscience, I shall see with sincere satisfaction the progress of those sentiments which tend to restore to man all his natural rights, convinced he has no natural right in opposition to his social duties.

I reciprocate your kind prayers for the protection & blessing of the common father and creator of man, and tender you for yourselves & your religious association, assurances of my high respect & esteem.

Th Jefferson

"Veto Act on Incorporating the Alexandria Protestant Episcopal Church," by *James Madison* (1811)

Although many people today think of the judiciary as the branch that is charged with interpreting the Constitution and making sure laws comply with it, James Madison saw a clear role for the president in that area. While serving in office, he acted on his belief that a president must respect the limits on religious establishment, including by using his veto—and explaining it. Here, he explains why he vetoed a law passed by Congress that would have given Washington, D.C., a formal role in a local Episcopal church, explaining that to do so would improperly entangle the government with a religious body.

Having examined and considered the Bill, entitled "An Act incorporating the protestant Episcopal Church in the Town of Alexandria in the District of Columbia," I now return the Bill to the House of Representatives, in which it originated, with the following objections.

Because the Bill exceeds the rightful authority, to which Governments are limited by the essential distinction between Civil and Religious functions, and violates, in particular, the Article of the Constitution of the United States which declares, that "Congress shall make no law respecting a Religious establishment." The Bill enacts into, and establishes by law, sundry rules and proceedings relative purely to the organization and polity of the Church incorporated, and comprehending even the election and removal of the Minister of the same, so that no change could be made therein, by the particular Society, or by the General Church of which it is a member, and whose authority it recognizes. This particular Church, therefore, would so far be a religious establishment by law, a legal force and sanction being given to certain articles in its constitution and administration. Nor can it be considered that the articles thus established, are to be taken as the descriptive criteria only, of the corporate identity of the Society, in as much as this identity, must depend on other characteristics, as the regulations established are generally unessential and alterable, according to the principles and cannons, by which Churches of that denomination govern themselves, and as the injunctions & prohibitions contained in the regulations would be enforced by the penal consequences applicable to a violation of them according to the local law.

Because the Bill vests in the said incorporated Church, an authority to provide for the support of the poor, and the education of poor children of the same, an authority, which being altogether superfluous if the provision is to be the result of pious charity, would be a precident for giving to religious Societies as such, a legal agency in carrying into effect a public and civil duty.

"Veto Message on Act of Relief for the Baptist Church," by *James Madison* (1811)

In this message, President Madison again exercises his veto power along with his power of persuasion to stop a law that would have provided government resources to support religion, in this case the granting of land to a Baptist church.

To the House of Representatives of the United States:

Having examined and considered the bill entitled "An act for the relief of Richard Tervin, William Coleman, Edwin Lewis, Samuel Mims, Joseph Wilson, and the Baptist Church at Salem Meeting House, in the Mississippi Territory," I now return the same to the House of representatives, in which it originated, with the following objection:

Because the bill in reserving a certain parcel of land of the United States for the use of said Baptist Church comprises a principle and precedent for the appropriation of funds of the United States for the use and support of religious societies, contrary to the article of the Constitution which declares that "Congress shall make no law respecting a religious establishment."

JAMES MADISON.

Lemon v. Kurtzman (1971)

> *This case is a definitive statement of a core component of the Supreme Court's Establishment Clause jurisprudence. Notice that the ruling does not assume there is or should be a "wall of separation" between church and state; rather, the Court delineates a three-pronged test for determining if a law has violated the Establishment Clause: The law's purpose must be secular, the law can neither advance nor harm religion as its primary effect, and the law cannot create an excessive entanglement between religion and government. In this case, the Court found that providing government funding for secular subjects in religious schools violated the third prong of excessive entanglement.*

MR. CHIEF JUSTICE BURGER delivered the opinion of the Court.

These two appeals raise questions as to Pennsylvania and Rhode Island statutes providing state aid to church-related elementary and secondary schools. Both statutes are challenged as violative of the Establishment and Free Exercise

Clauses of the First Amendment and the Due Process Clause of the Fourteenth Amendment.

Pennsylvania has adopted a statutory program that provides financial support to nonpublic elementary and secondary schools by way of reimbursement for the cost of teachers' salaries, textbooks, and instructional materials in specified secular subjects. Rhode Island has adopted a statute under which the State pays directly to teachers in nonpublic elementary schools a supplement of 15% of their annual salary. Under each statute, state aid has been given to church-related educational institutions. We hold that both statutes are unconstitutional. . . .

II

. . . The language of the Religion Clauses of the First Amendment is, at best, opaque, particularly when compared with other portions of the Amendment. Its authors did not simply prohibit the establishment of a state church or a state religion, an area history shows they regarded as very important and fraught with great dangers. Instead, they commanded that there should be "no law respecting an establishment of religion." A law may be one "respecting" the forbidden objective while falling short of its total realization. A law "respecting" the proscribed result, that is, the establishment of religion, is not always easily identifiable as one violative of the Clause. A given law might not establish a state religion, but nevertheless be one "respecting" that end in the sense of being a step that could lead to such establishment, and hence offend the First Amendment.

In the absence of precisely stated constitutional prohibitions, we must draw lines with reference to the three main evils against which the Establishment Clause was intended to afford protection: "sponsorship, financial support, and active involvement of the sovereign in religious activity."

Every analysis in this area must begin with consideration of the cumulative criteria developed by the Court over many years. Three such tests may be gleaned from our cases. First, the statute must have a secular legislative purpose; second, its principal or primary effect must be one that neither advances nor inhibits religion; finally, the statute must not foster "an excessive government entanglement with religion."

Inquiry into the legislative purposes of the Pennsylvania and Rhode Island statutes affords no basis for a conclusion that the legislative intent was to advance religion. On the contrary, the statutes themselves clearly state that they are intended to enhance the quality of the secular education in all schools covered by the compulsory attendance laws. There is no reason to believe the legislatures meant anything else. A State always has a legitimate concern for maintaining minimum standards in all schools it allows to operate. . . . [W]e find nothing here that undermines the stated legislative intent; it must therefore be accorded appropriate deference. . . .

III

. . . Our prior holdings do not call for total separation between church and state; total separation is not possible in an absolute sense. Some relationship between government and religious organizations is inevitable. . . .

. . . In order to determine whether the government entanglement with religion is excessive, we must examine the character and purposes of the institutions that are benefited, the nature of the aid that the State provides, and the resulting relationship between the government and the religious authority. . . . Here we find that both statutes foster an impermissible degree of entanglement.

(a) Rhode Island program

The District Court made extensive findings on the grave potential for excessive entanglement that inheres in the religious character and purpose of the Roman Catholic elementary schools of Rhode Island, to date the sole beneficiaries of the Rhode Island Salary Supplement Act. . . .

The church schools involved in the program are located close to parish churches. . . . Although only approximately 30 minutes a day are devoted to direct religious instruction, there are religiously oriented extracurricular activities. Approximately two-thirds of the teachers in these schools are nuns of various religious orders. Their dedicated efforts provide an atmosphere in which religious instruction and religious vocations are natural and proper parts of life in such schools. Indeed, as the District Court found, the role of teaching nuns in enhancing the religious atmosphere has led the parochial school authorities to attempt to maintain a one-to-one ratio between nuns and lay teachers in all schools, rather than to permit some to be staffed almost entirely by lay teachers. . . .

. . . In short, parochial schools involve substantial religious activity and purpose. . . .

The schools are governed by the standards set forth in a "Handbook of School Regulations," which has the force of synodal law in the diocese. It emphasizes the role and importance of the teacher in parochial schools . . .

The Handbook also states that: "Religious formation is not confined to formal courses; nor is it restricted to a single subject area." Finally, the Handbook advises teachers to stimulate interest in religious vocations and missionary work. Given the mission of the church school, these instructions are consistent and logical. . . .

. . . [W]hat has been recounted suggests the potential, if not actual, hazards of this form of state aid. The teacher is employed by a religious organization, subject to the direction and discipline of religious authorities, and works in a system dedicated to rearing children in a particular faith. These controls are not lessened by the fact that most of the lay teachers are of the Catholic faith. Inevitably, some of a teacher's responsibilities hover on the border between secular and religious orientation.

We need not and do not assume that teachers in parochial schools will be guilty of bad faith or any conscious design to evade the limitations imposed by the statute and the First Amendment. We simply recognize that a dedicated religious person, teaching in a school affiliated with his or her faith and operated to inculcate its tenets, will inevitably experience great difficulty in remaining religiously neutral. Doctrines and faith are not inculcated or advanced by neutrals. With the best of intentions, such a teacher would find it hard to make a total separation between secular teaching and religious doctrine. What would appear to some to be essential to good citizenship might well for others border on or constitute instruction in religion. Further difficulties are inherent in the combination of religious discipline and the possibility of disagreement between teacher and religious authorities over the meaning of the statutory restrictions.

We do not assume, however, that parochial school teachers will be unsuccessful in their attempts to segregate their religious belief from their secular educational responsibilities. But the potential for impermissible fostering of religion is present. . . . The State must be certain, given the Religion Clauses, that subsidized teachers do not inculcate religion—indeed, the State here has undertaken to do so. To ensure that no trespass occurs, the State has therefore carefully conditioned its aid with pervasive restrictions. . . .

A comprehensive, discriminating, and continuing state surveillance will inevitably be required to ensure that these restrictions are obeyed and the First Amendment otherwise respected. Unlike a book, a teacher cannot be inspected once so as to determine the extent and intent of his or her personal beliefs and subjective acceptance of the limitations imposed by the First Amendment. These prophylactic contacts will involve excessive and enduring entanglement between state and church.

There is another area of entanglement in the Rhode Island program that gives concern. The statute excludes teachers employed by nonpublic schools whose average per-pupil expenditures on secular education equal or exceed the comparable figures for public schools. In the event that the total expenditures of an otherwise eligible school exceed this norm, the program requires the government to examine the school's records in order to determine how much of the total expenditures is attributable to secular education and how much to religious activity. This kind of state inspection and evaluation of the religious content of a religious organization is fraught with the sort of entanglement that the Constitution forbids. It is a relationship pregnant with dangers of excessive government direction of church schools, and hence of churches. The Court noted "the hazards of government supporting churches" in *Walz v. Tax Commission*, and we cannot ignore here the danger that pervasive modern governmental power will ultimately intrude on religion and thus conflict with the Religion Clauses.

(b) Pennsylvania program

The Pennsylvania statute also provides state aid to church-related schools for teachers' salaries. The complaint describes an educational system that is very similar to the one existing in Rhode Island. According to the allegations, the church-related elementary and secondary schools are controlled by religious organizations, have the purpose of propagating and promoting a particular religious faith, and conduct their operations to fulfill that purpose. . . .

As we noted earlier, the very restrictions and surveillance necessary to ensure that teachers play a strictly nonideological role give rise to entanglements between church and state. The Pennsylvania statute, like that of Rhode Island, fosters this kind of relationship. Reimbursement is not only limited to courses offered in the public schools and materials approved by state officials, but the statute excludes "any subject matter expressing religious teaching, or the morals or forms of worship of any sect." In addition, schools seeking reimbursement must maintain accounting procedures that require the State to establish the cost of the secular, as distinguished from the religious, instruction.

The Pennsylvania statute, moreover, has the further defect of providing state financial aid directly to the church-related school. . . . In *Walz v. Tax Commission*, the Court warned of the dangers of direct payments to religious organizations:

> Obviously a direct money subsidy would be a relationship pregnant with involvement and, as with most governmental grant programs, could encompass sustained and detailed administrative relationships for enforcement of statutory or administrative standards. . . .

The history of government grants of a continuing cash subsidy indicates that such programs have almost always been accompanied by varying measures of control and surveillance. The government cash grants before us now provide no basis for predicting that comprehensive measures of surveillance and controls will not follow. In particular, the government's post-audit power to inspect and evaluate a church-related school's financial records and to determine which expenditures are religious and which are secular creates an intimate and continuing relationship between church and state.

IV

A broader base of entanglement of yet a different character is presented by the divisive political potential of these state programs. In a community where such a large number of pupils are served by church-related schools, it can be assumed that state assistance will entail considerable political activity. Partisans of parochial schools, understandably concerned with rising costs and sincerely dedicated to both the religious and secular educational missions of their schools, will inevitably champion this cause and promote political action to achieve their goals. Those who oppose state aid, whether for constitutional, religious, or fiscal reasons, will inevitably respond and employ all of the usual political campaign techniques to prevail. Candidates will be forced to declare, and voters to choose. It would be unrealistic to ignore the fact that many people confronted with issues of this kind will find their votes aligned with their faith.

Ordinarily, political debate and division, however vigorous or even partisan, are normal and healthy manifestations of our democratic system of government, but political division along religious lines was one of the principal evils against which the First Amendment was intended to protect. The potential divisiveness of such conflict is a threat to the normal political process. To have States or communities divide on the issues presented by state aid to parochial schools would tend to confuse and obscure other issues of great urgency. We have an expanding array of vexing issues, local and national, domestic and international, to debate and divide on. It conflicts with our whole history and tradition to permit questions of the Religion Clauses to assume such importance in our legislatures and in our elections that they could divert attention from the myriad issues and problems that confront every level of government. The highways of church and state relationships are not likely to be one-way streets, and the Constitution's authors sought to protect religious worship from the pervasive power of government. The history of many countries attests to the hazards of religion's intruding into the political arena or of political power intruding into the legitimate and free exercise of religious belief. . . .

The potential for political divisiveness related to religious belief and practice is aggravated in these two statutory programs by the need for continuing annual appropriations and the likelihood of larger and larger demands as costs and populations grow. . . .

Finally, nothing we have said can be construed to disparage the role of church-related elementary and secondary schools in our national life. Their contribution has been and is enormous. Nor do we ignore their economic plight in a period of rising costs and expanding need. Taxpayers generally have been spared vast sums by the maintenance of these educational institutions by religious organizations, largely by the gifts of faithful adherents.

The merit and benefits of these schools, however, are not the issue before us in these cases. The sole question is whether state aid to these schools can be squared with the dictates of the Religion Clauses. Under our system, the choice has been made that government is to be entirely excluded from the area of religious instruction, and churches excluded from the affairs of government. The Constitution decrees that religion must be a private matter for the individual, the family, and the institutions of private choice, and that, while some involvement and entanglement are inevitable, lines must be drawn.

The judgment of the Rhode Island District Court in No. 569 and No. 570 is affirmed. The judgment of the Pennsylvania District Court in No. 89 is reversed, and the case is remanded for further proceedings consistent with this opinion.

Lynch v. Donnelly (1984)

> In this case, the Court attempted to grapple with the
> question of when religious displays were appropriate in
> public spaces. Justice O'Connor's concurrence lays out
> what is called the "Endorsement Test," which she uses to
> argue that the city of Pawtucket's display of a nativity
> scene, along with a Christmas tree and a Santa Claus
> model, was allowable because it was not an endorsement
> of a particular religion.

CHIEF JUSTICE BURGER delivered the opinion of the
Court.

We granted certiorari to decide whether the Establishment Clause of the First Amendment prohibits a municipal-
ity from including a creche, or Nativity scene, in its annual
Christmas display.

I

Each year, in cooperation with the downtown retail merchants' association, the city of Pawtucket, R.I., erects a Christmas display as part of its observance of the Christmas holiday season. The display is situated in a park owned by a nonprofit organization and located in the heart of the shopping district. The display is essentially like those to be found in hundreds of towns or cities across the Nation—often on public grounds—during the Christmas season. The Pawtucket display comprises many of the figures and decorations traditionally associated with Christmas, including, among other things, a Santa Claus house, reindeer pulling Santa's sleigh, candy-striped poles, a Christmas tree, carolers, cutout figures representing such characters as a clown, an elephant, and a teddy bear, hundreds of colored lights, a large banner that reads "SEASONS GREETINGS," and the creche at issue here. All components of this display are owned by the city.

The creche, which has been included in the display for 40 or more years, consists of the traditional figures, including the Infant Jesus, Mary and Joseph, angels, shepherds, kings, and animals, all ranging in height from 5" to 5'. In 1973, when the present creche was acquired, it cost the city $1,365; it now is valued at $200. The erection and dismantling of the creche costs the city about $20 per year; nominal expenses are incurred in lighting the creche. No money has been expended on its maintenance for the past 10 years.

Respondents, Pawtucket residents and individual members of the Rhode Island affiliate of the American Civil Liberties Union, and the affiliate itself, brought this action in the United States District Court for Rhode Island, challenging the city's inclusion of the creche in the annual display. The District Court held that the city's inclusion of the creche in the display violates the Establishment Clause, which is binding on the states through the Fourteenth Amendment. . . .

A divided panel of the Court of Appeals for the First Circuit affirmed. We granted certiorari, and we reverse.

II

A

In every Establishment Clause case, we must reconcile the inescapable tension between the objective of preventing unnecessary intrusion of either the church or the state upon the other, and the reality that, as the Court has so often noted, total separation of the two is not possible.

The Court has sometimes described the Religion Clauses as erecting a "wall" between church and state. . . . The metaphor has served as a reminder that the Establishment Clause forbids an established church or anything approaching it. But the metaphor itself is not a wholly accurate description of the practical aspects of the relationship that in fact exists between church and state.

No significant segment of our society, and no institution within it, can exist in a vacuum or in total or absolute isolation from all the other parts, much less from government. . . . Nor does the Constitution require complete separation of church and state; it affirmatively mandates accommodation, not merely tolerance, of all religions, and forbids hostility toward any. Anything less would require the "callous indifference" we have said was never intended by the Establishment Clause. Indeed, we have observed, such hostility would bring us into "war with our national tradition as embodied in the First Amendment's guaranty of the free exercise of religion."

B

The Court's interpretation of the Establishment Clause has comported with what history reveals was the contemporaneous understanding of its guarantees. A significant example of the contemporaneous understanding of that Clause is found in the events of the first week of the First Session of the First Congress in 1789. In the very week that Congress approved the Establishment Clause as part of the Bill of Rights for submission to the states, it enacted legislation providing for paid Chaplains for the House and Senate. In *Marsh v. Chambers* (1983), we noted that 17 Members of that First Congress had been Delegates to the Constitutional Convention where freedom of speech, press, and religion and antagonism toward an established church were subjects of frequent discussion. . . .

The interpretation of the Establishment Clause by Congress in 1789 takes on special significance in light of the Court's emphasis that the First Congress "was a Congress whose constitutional decisions have always been regarded, as they should be regarded, as of the greatest weight in the interpretation of that fundamental instrument. . . ." It is clear that neither the 17 draftsmen of the Constitution who were Members of the First Congress, nor the Congress of 1789, saw any establishment problem in the employment of congressional Chaplains to offer daily prayers in the Congress, a practice that has continued for nearly two centuries. It would be difficult to identify a more striking example of the accommodation of religious belief intended by the Framers.

C

There is an unbroken history of official acknowledgment by all three branches of government of the role of religion in American life from at least 1789. . . .

Our history is replete with official references to the value and invocation of Divine guidance in deliberations and pro-nouncements of the Founding Fathers and contemporary leaders. . . . President Washington and his successors pro-claimed Thanksgiving, with all its religious overtones, a day of national celebration and Congress made it a National Hol-iday more than a century ago. That holiday has not lost its theme of expressing thanks for Divine aid any more than has Christmas lost its religious significance.

Executive Orders and other official announcements of Presidents and of the Congress have proclaimed both Christ-mas and Thanksgiving National Holidays in religious terms. And, by Acts of Congress, it has long been the practice that federal employees are released from duties on these National Holidays, while being paid from the same public revenues that provide the compensation of the Chaplains of the Senate and the House and the military services. Thus, it is clear that Gov-ernment has long recognized—indeed it has subsidized—holidays with religious significance.

Other examples of reference to our religious heritage are found in the statutorily prescribed national motto "In God We Trust," which Congress and the President mandated for our currency, and in the language "One nation under God," as part of the Pledge of Allegiance to the American flag. That pledge is recited by many thousands of public school children—and adults every year.

Art galleries supported by public revenues display religious paintings of the 15th and 16th centuries, predominantly inspired by one religious faith. The National Gallery in Washington, maintained with Government support, for example, has long exhibited masterpieces with religious messages, notably the Last Supper, and paintings depicting the Birth of Christ, the Crucifixion, and the Resurrection, among many others with explicit Christian themes and messages. The very chamber in which oral arguments on this case were heard is decorated with a notable and permanent—not seasonal— symbol of religion: Moses with the Ten Commandments. Congress has long provided chapels in the Capitol for religious worship and meditation.

There are countless other illustrations of the Government's acknowledgment of our religious heritage and governmental sponsorship of graphic manifestations of that heritage. Congress has directed the President to proclaim a National Day of Prayer each year "on which [day] the people of the United States may turn to God in prayer and meditation at churches, in groups, and as individuals." Our Presidents have repeatedly issued such Proclamations. Presidential Proclamations and messages have also been issued to commemorate Jewish Heritage Week and the Jewish High Holy Days. One cannot look at even this brief resume without finding that our history is pervaded by expressions of religious beliefs such as are found in *Zorach*. Equally pervasive is the evidence of accommodation of all faiths and all forms of religious expression, and hostility toward none. . . .

III

This history may help explain why the Court consistently has declined to take a rigid, absolutist view of the Establishment Clause.... In our modern, complex society, whose traditions and constitutional underpinnings rest on and encourage diversity and pluralism in all areas, an absolutist approach in applying the Establishment Clause is simplistic, and has been uniformly rejected by the Court.

Rather than mechanically invalidating all governmental conduct or statutes that confer benefits or give special recognition to religion in general or to one faith—as an absolutist approach would dictate—the Court has scrutinized challenged legislation or official conduct to determine whether, in reality, it establishes a religion or religious faith, or tends to do so. ...

In each case, the inquiry calls for line-drawing; no fixed, *per se* rule can be framed. The Establishment Clause, like the Due Process Clauses, is not a precise, detailed provision in a legal code capable of ready application. ...

In the line-drawing process, we have often found it useful to inquire whether the challenged law or conduct has a secular purpose, whether its principal or primary effect is to advance or inhibit religion, and whether it creates an excessive entanglement of government with religion. But we have repeatedly emphasized our unwillingness to be confined to any single test or criterion in this sensitive area. ...

In this case, the focus of our inquiry must be on the creche in the context of the Christmas season. ...

... When viewed in the proper context of the Christmas Holiday season, it is apparent that, on this record, there is insufficient evidence to establish that the inclusion of the creche is a purposeful or surreptitious effort to express some kind of subtle governmental advocacy of a particular religious message. In a pluralistic society, a variety of motives and purposes are implicated. The city, like the Congresses and Presidents, however, has principally taken note of a significant historical religious event long celebrated in the Western World. The creche in the display depicts the historical origins of this traditional event long recognized as a National Holiday.

The narrow question is whether there is a secular purpose for Pawtucket's display of the creche. The display is sponsored by the city to celebrate the Holiday and to depict the origins of that Holiday. These are legitimate secular purposes. The District Court's inference, drawn from the religious nature of the creche, that the city has no secular purpose was, on this record, clearly erroneous. . . .

The dissent asserts some observers may perceive that the city has aligned itself with the Christian faith by including a Christian symbol in its display, and that this serves to advance religion. We can assume . . . that the display advances religion in a sense; but our precedents plainly contemplate that, on occasion, some advancement of religion will result from governmental action. . . . *Here, whatever benefit there is to one faith or religion or to all religions, is indirect, remote, and incidental; display of the creche is no more an advancement or endorsement of religion than the Congressional and Executive recognition of the origins of the Holiday itself as "Christ's Mass," or the exhibition of literally hundreds of religious paintings in governmentally supported museums.*

The District Court found that there had been no administrative entanglement between religion and state resulting from the city's ownership and use of the creche. But it went on to hold that some political divisiveness was engendered by this litigation. Coupled with its finding of an impermissible sectarian purpose and effect, this persuaded the court that there was "excessive entanglement." . . .

. . . In this case . . . there is no reason to disturb the District Court's finding on the absence of administrative entanglement. . . . In many respects, the display requires far less ongoing, day-to-day interaction between church and state than religious paintings in public galleries. There is nothing here, of course, like the "comprehensive, discriminating, and continuing state surveillance" or the "enduring entanglement" present in *Lemon*.

The Court of Appeals correctly observed that this Court has not held that political divisiveness alone can serve to invalidate otherwise permissible conduct. And we decline to so hold today. . . . [A]part from this litigation, there is no evidence of political friction or divisiveness over the creche in the 40-year history of Pawtucket's Christmas celebration. The District Court stated that the inclusion of the creche for the 40 years has been "marked by no apparent dissension," and that the display has had a "calm history." Curiously, it went on to hold that the political divisiveness engendered by this lawsuit was evidence of excessive entanglement. A litigant cannot, by the very act of commencing a lawsuit, however, create the appearance of divisiveness and then exploit it as evidence of entanglement.

We are satisfied that the city has a secular purpose for including the creche, that the city has not impermissibly advanced religion, and that including the creche does not create excessive entanglement between religion and government.

IV

JUSTICE BRENNAN describes the creche as a "re-creation of an event that lies at the heart of Christian faith." . . .

Of course, the creche is identified with one religious faith, but no more so than the examples we have set out from prior cases in which we found no conflict with the Establishment Clause. It would be ironic, however, if the inclusion of a single symbol of a particular historic religious event, as part of a celebration acknowledged in the Western World for 20 centuries, and in this country by the people, by the Executive Branch, by the Congress, and the courts for 2 centuries, would so "taint" the city's exhibit as to render it violative of the Establishment Clause. To forbid the use of this one passive symbol—the creche—at the very time people are taking note of the season with Christmas hymns and carols in public schools and other public places, and while the Congress and legislatures open sessions with prayers by paid chaplains, would be a stilted overreaction contrary to our history and to our holdings. If the presence of the creche in this display violates the Establishment Clause, a host of other forms of taking official note of Christmas, and of our religious heritage, are equally offensive to the Constitution. . . .

VI

We hold that, notwithstanding the religious significance of the creche, the city of Pawtucket has not violated the Establishment Clause of the First Amendment. Accordingly, the judgment of the Court of Appeals is reversed.

It is so ordered.

... JUSTICE O'CONNOR, concurring.

The Establishment Clause prohibits government from making adherence to a religion relevant in any way to a person's standing in the political community. Government can run afoul of that prohibition in two principal ways. One is excessive entanglement with religious institutions, which may interfere with the independence of the institutions, give the institutions access to government or governmental powers not fully shared by nonadherents of the religion, and foster the creation of political constituencies defined along religious lines. The second and more direct infringement is government endorsement or disapproval of religion. Endorsement sends a message to nonadherents that they are outsiders, not full members of the political community, and an accompanying message to adherents that they are insiders, favored members of the political community. Disapproval sends the opposite message.

Our prior cases have used the three-part test articulated in *Lemon v. Kurtzman*, as a guide to detecting these two forms of unconstitutional government action. It has never been entirely clear, however, how the three parts of the test relate to the principles enshrined in the Establishment Clause. Focusing on institutional entanglement and on endorsement or disapproval of religion clarifies the *Lemon* test as an analytical device. . . .

The central issue in this case is whether Pawtucket has endorsed Christianity by its display of the creche. To answer that question, we must examine both what Pawtucket intended to communicate in displaying the creche and what message the city's display actually conveyed. The purpose and effect prongs of the *Lemon* test represent these two aspects of the meaning of the city's action.

The meaning of a statement to its audience depends both on the intention of the speaker and on the "objective" meaning of the statement in the community. Some listeners need not rely solely on the words themselves in discerning the speaker's intent: they can judge the intent by, for example, examining the context of the statement or asking questions of the speaker. Other listeners do not have or will not seek access to such evidence of intent. They will rely instead on the words themselves; for them, the message actually conveyed may be something not actually intended. If the audience is large, as it always is when government "speaks" by word or deed, some portion of the audience will inevitably receive a message determined by the "objective" content of the statement, and some portion will inevitably receive the intended message. Examination of both the subjective and the objective components of the message communicated by a government action is therefore necessary to determine whether the action carries a forbidden meaning.

The purpose prong of the *Lemon* test asks whether government's actual purpose is to endorse or disapprove of religion. The effect prong asks whether, irrespective of government's actual purpose, the practice under review in fact conveys a message of endorsement or disapproval. An affirmative answer to either question should render the challenged practice invalid.

The purpose prong of the *Lemon* test requires that a government activity have a secular purpose. That requirement is not satisfied, however, by the mere existence of some secular purpose, however dominated by religious purposes. In *Stone v. Graham*, for example, the Court held that posting copies of the Ten Commandments in schools violated the purpose prong of the *Lemon* test, yet the State plainly had some secular objectives, such as instilling most of the values of the

Ten Commandments and illustrating their connection to our legal system. The proper inquiry under the purpose prong of *Lemon*, I submit, is whether the government intends to convey a message of endorsement or disapproval of religion.

Applying that formulation to this case, I would find that Pawtucket did not intend to convey any message of endorsement of Christianity or disapproval of non-Christian religions. The evident purpose of including the creche in the larger display was not promotion of the religious content of the creche, but celebration of the public holiday through its traditional symbols. Celebration of public holidays, which have cultural significance even if they also have religious aspects, is a legitimate secular purpose.

The District Court's finding that the display of the creche had no secular purpose was based on erroneous reasoning. The District Court believed that it should ascertain the city's purpose in displaying the creche separate and apart from the general purpose in setting up the display. It also found that, because the tradition-celebrating purpose was suspect in the court's eyes, the city's use of an unarguably religious symbol "raises an inference" of intent to endorse. When viewed in light of correct legal principles, the District Court's finding of unlawful purpose was clearly erroneous.

Focusing on the evil of government endorsement or disapproval of religion makes clear that the effect prong of the *Lemon* test is properly interpreted not to require invalidation of a government practice merely because it in fact causes, even as a primary effect, advancement or inhibition of religion. The laws upheld in *Walz v. Tax Comm'n* (tax exemption for religious, educational, and charitable organizations), in *McGowan v. Maryland* (mandatory Sunday closing law), and in *Zorach v. Clauson* (released time from school for off-campus religious instruction), had such effects, but they did not violate the Establishment Clause. What is crucial is that a government practice not have the effect of communicating a message of government endorsement or disapproval of religion. It is only practices having that effect, whether intentionally or unintentionally, that make religion relevant, in reality or public perception, to status in the political community.

Pawtucket's display of its creche, I believe, does not communicate a message that the government intends to endorse the Christian beliefs represented by the creche. Although the religious and indeed sectarian significance of the creche, as the District Court found, is not neutralized by the setting, the overall holiday setting changes what viewers may fairly understand to be the purpose of the display—as a typical museum setting, though not neutralizing the religious content of a religious painting, negates any message of endorsement of that content. The display celebrates a public holiday, and no one contends that declaration of that holiday is understood to be an endorsement of religion. The holiday itself has very strong secular components and traditions. Government celebration of the holiday, which is extremely common, generally is not understood to endorse the religious content of the holiday, just as government celebration of Thanksgiving is not so understood. The creche is a traditional symbol of the holiday that is very commonly displayed along with purely secular symbols, as it was in Pawtucket.

These features combine to make the government's display of the creche in this particular physical setting no more an endorsement of religion than such governmental "acknowledgments" of religion as legislative prayers of the type approved in *Marsh v. Chambers*, government declaration of Thanksgiving as a public holiday, printing of "In God We Trust" on coins, and opening court sessions with "God save the United States and this honorable court." Those government acknowledgments of religion serve, in the only ways reasonably possible in our culture, the legitimate secular purposes of solemnizing public occasions, expressing confidence in the future, and encouraging the recognition of what is worthy of appreciation in society. For that reason, and because of their history and ubiquity, those practices are not understood as conveying government approval of particular religious beliefs. The display of the creche likewise serves a secular purpose—celebration of a public holiday with traditional symbols. It cannot fairly be understood to convey a message of government endorsement of religion. It is significant in this regard that the creche display apparently caused no political divisiveness prior to the filing of this lawsuit, although Pawtucket had incorporated the creche in its annual Christmas display for some years. For these reasons, I conclude that Pawtucket's display of the creche does not have the effect of communicating endorsement of Christianity.

County of Allegheny v. ACLU, Greater Pittsburgh Chapter (1989)

In this case, the Court revisited the issue of public religious displays, focusing on a display of a nativity scene inside a courthouse, along with a separate display of a menorah and a Christmas tree outside a city building. This time, the Court ruled that the nativity scene was an endorsement of Christianity and thus violated the Establishment Clause, but that the menorah and Christmas tree display was constitutionally permissible. Many would argue that the Court here was doing what Madison demanded: preventing government from favoring one religion over another, while not banning entirely the presence of religion in public life. To others, however, this ruling was an overreach, an unjust restriction on the role religion should play in public spaces.

JUSTICE HARRY BLACKMUN . . . delivered the opinion of the Court.

This litigation concerns the constitutionality of two recurring holiday displays located on public property in downtown Pittsburgh. The first is a creche placed on the Grand Staircase of the Allegheny County Courthouse. The second is a Chanukah menorah placed just outside the City-County

Building, next to a Christmas tree and a sign saluting liberty. The Court of Appeals for the Third Circuit ruled that each display violates the Establishment Clause of the First Amendment because each has the impermissible effect of endorsing religion.

We agree that the creche display has that unconstitutional effect, but reverse the Court of Appeals' judgment regarding the menorah display.

I

A

The county courthouse is owned by Allegheny County and is its seat of government. It houses the offices of the county commissioners, controller, treasurer, sheriff, and clerk of court. Civil and criminal trials are held there. The "main," "most beautiful," and "most public" part of the courthouse is its Grand Staircase, set into one arch and surrounded by others, with arched windows serving as a backdrop. . . .

The creche in the county courthouse, like other creches, is a visual representation of the scene in the manger in Bethlehem shortly after the birth of Jesus, as described in the Gospels of Luke and Matthew. The creche includes figures of the infant Jesus, Mary, Joseph, farm animals, shepherds, and wise men, all placed in or before a wooden representation of a manger, which has at its crest an angel bearing a banner that proclaims "Gloria in Excelsis Deo!" . . .

B

The City-County Building is separate and a block removed from the county courthouse and, as the name implies, is jointly owned by the city of Pittsburgh and Allegheny County. The city's portion of the building houses the city's principal offices, including the mayor's. The city is responsible for the building's Grant Street entrance, which has three rounded arches supported by columns.

For a number of years, the city has had a large Christmas tree under the middle arch outside the Grant Street entrance. Following this practice, city employees, on November 17, 1986, erected a 45-foot tree under the middle arch and decorated it with lights and ornaments. A few days later, the city placed at the foot of the tree a sign bearing the mayor's name and entitled "Salute to Liberty." Beneath the title, the sign stated:

"During this holiday season, the city of Pittsburgh salutes liberty. Let these festive lights remind us that we are the keepers of the flame of liberty and our legacy of freedom."

At least since 1982, the city has expanded its Grant Street holiday display to include a symbolic representation of Chanukah, an 8-day Jewish holiday that begins on the 25th day of the Jewish lunar month of Kislev. The 25th of Kislev usually occurs in December, and thus Chanukah is the annual Jewish holiday that falls closest to Christmas Day each year. . . .

On December 22 of the 1986 holiday season, the city placed at the Grant Street entrance to the City-County Building an 18-foot Chanukah menorah of an abstract tree-and-branch design. The menorah was placed next to the city's 45-foot Christmas tree, against one of the columns that supports the arch into which the tree was set. The menorah is owned by Chabad, a Jewish group, but is stored, erected, and removed each year by the city. The tree, the sign, and the menorah were all removed on January 13. . . .

II

. . . Respondents claim that the displays of the creche and the menorah each violate the Establishment Clause of the First Amendment, made applicable to state governments by the Fourteenth Amendment. . . .

III

A

This Nation is heir to a history and tradition of religious diversity that dates from the settlement of the North American Continent. Sectarian differences among various Christian denominations were central to the origins of our Republic. Since then, adherents of religions too numerous to name have made the United States their home, as have those whose beliefs expressly exclude religion.

Precisely because of the religious diversity that is our national heritage, the Founders added to the Constitution a Bill of Rights, the very first words of which declare: "Congress shall make no law respecting an establishment of religion, or prohibiting the free exercise thereof. . . ." Perhaps in the early days of the Republic these words were understood to protect only the diversity within Christianity, but today they are recognized as guaranteeing religious liberty and equality to "the infidel, the atheist, or the adherent of a non-Christian faith such as Islam or Judaism." It is settled law that no government official in this Nation may violate these fundamental constitutional rights regarding matters of conscience.

In the course of adjudicating specific cases, this Court has come to understand the Establishment Clause to mean that government may not promote or affiliate itself with any religious doctrine or organization, may not discriminate among persons on the basis of their religious beliefs and practices, may not delegate a governmental power to a religious institution, and may not involve itself too deeply in such an institution's affairs. . . .

B

. . . We have had occasion in the past to apply Establishment Clause principles to the government's display of objects with religious significance. In *Stone v. Graham* (1980), we held that the display of a copy of the Ten Commandments on the walls of public classrooms violates the Establishment Clause. Closer to the facts of this litigation is *Lynch v. Donnelly*, in which we considered whether the city of Pawtucket, R.I., had violated the Establishment Clause by including a creche in its annual Christmas display, located in a private park within the downtown shopping district. . . .

The rationale of the majority opinion in *Lynch* is none too clear: the opinion contains two strands, neither of which provides guidance for decision in subsequent cases. First, the opinion states that the inclusion of the creche in the display was "no more an advancement or endorsement of religion" than other "endorsements" this Court has approved in the past, but the opinion offers no discernible measure for distinguishing between permissible and impermissible endorsements. Second, the opinion observes that any benefit the government's display of the creche gave to religion was no more than "indirect, remote, and incidental,"—without saying how or why. . . .

. . . [D]espite divergence at the bottom line, the five Justices in concurrence and dissent in *Lynch* agreed upon the relevant constitutional principles: the government's use of religious symbolism is unconstitutional if it has the effect of endorsing religious beliefs, and the effect of the government's use of religious symbolism depends upon its context. These general principles are sound, and have been adopted by the Court in subsequent cases. . . .

Accordingly, our present task is to determine whether the display of the creche and the menorah, in their respective "particular physical settings," has the effect of endorsing or disapproving religious beliefs.

IV

We turn first to the county's creche display. There is no doubt, of course, that the creche itself is capable of communicating a religious message. Indeed, the creche in this lawsuit uses words, as well as the picture of the nativity scene, to make its religious meaning unmistakably clear. "Glory to God in the Highest!" says the angel in the creche—Glory to God because of the birth of Jesus. This praise to God in Christian terms is indisputably religious—indeed sectarian—just as it is when said in the Gospel or in a church service.

Under the Court's holding in *Lynch*, the effect of a creche display turns on its setting. Here, unlike in *Lynch*, nothing in the context of the display detracts from the creche's religious message. The *Lynch* display comprised a series of figures and objects, each group of which had its own focal point. Santa's house and his reindeer were objects of attention separate from the creche, and had their specific visual story to tell. Similarly, whatever a "talking" wishing well may be, it obviously was a center of attention separate from the creche. Here, in contrast, the creche stands alone: it is the single element of the display on the Grand Staircase. . . .

Nor does the fact that the creche was the setting for the county's annual Christmas carol program diminish its religious meaning. First, the carol program in 1986 lasted only from December 3 to December 23, and occupied, at most, one hour a day. The effect of the creche on those who viewed it when the choirs were not singing—the vast majority of the time—cannot be negated by the presence of the choir program. Second, because some of the carols performed at the site of the creche were religious in nature, those carols were more likely to augment the religious quality of the scene than to secularize it.

Furthermore, the creche sits on the Grand Staircase, the "main" and "most beautiful part" of the building that is the seat of county government. No viewer could reasonably think that it occupies this location without the support and approval of the government. Thus, by permitting the "display of the creche in this particular physical setting," the county sends an unmistakable message that it supports and promotes the Christian praise to God that is the creche's religious message.

The fact that the creche bears a sign disclosing its ownership by a Roman Catholic organization does not alter this conclusion. On the contrary, the sign simply demonstrates that the government is endorsing the religious message of that organization, rather than communicating a message of its own. But the Establishment Clause does not limit only the religious content of the government's own communications. It also prohibits the government's support and promotion of religious communications by religious organizations. Indeed, the very concept of "endorsement" conveys the sense of promoting someone else's message. Thus, by prohibiting government endorsement of religion, the Establishment Clause prohibits precisely what occurred here: the government's lending its support to the communication of a religious organization's religious message.

Finally, the county argues that it is sufficient to validate the display of the creche on the Grand Staircase that the display celebrates Christmas, and Christmas is a national holiday. This argument obviously proves too much. It would allow the celebration of the Eucharist inside a courthouse on Christmas Eve. While the county may have doubts about the constitutional status of celebrating the Eucharist inside the courthouse under the government's auspices, this Court does not. The government may acknowledge Christmas as a cultural phenomenon, but, under the First Amendment, it may not observe it as a Christian holy day by suggesting that people praise God for the birth of Jesus.

In sum, *Lynch* teaches that government may celebrate Christmas in some manner and form, but not in a way that endorses Christian doctrine. Here, Allegheny County has transgressed this line. It has chosen to celebrate Christmas in a way that has the effect of endorsing a patently Christian message: Glory to God for the birth of Jesus Christ. Under *Lynch*, and the rest of our cases, nothing more is required to demonstrate a violation of the Establishment Clause. The display of the creche in this context, therefore, must be permanently enjoined. . . .

VI

The display of the Chanukah menorah in front of the City-County Building may well present a closer constitutional question. The menorah, one must recognize, is a religious symbol: it serves to commemorate the miracle of the oil as described in the Talmud. But the menorah's message is not exclusively religious. The menorah is the primary visual symbol for a holiday that, like Christmas, has both religious and secular dimensions.

Moreover, the menorah here stands next to a Christmas tree and a sign saluting liberty. While no challenge has been made here to the display of the tree and the sign, their presence is obviously relevant in determining the effect of the menorah's display. The necessary result of placing a menorah next to a Christmas tree is to create an "overall holiday setting" that represents both Christmas and Chanukah—two holidays, not one. . . .

Accordingly, the relevant question for Establishment Clause purposes is whether the combined display of the tree, the sign, and the menorah has the effect of endorsing both Christian and Jewish faiths, or rather simply recognizes that both Christmas and Chanukah are part of the same winter holiday season, which has attained a secular status in our society. Of the two interpretations of this particular display, the latter seems far more plausible, and is also in line with *Lynch*.

The Christmas tree, unlike the menorah, is not itself a religious symbol. Although Christmas trees once carried religious connotations, today they typify the secular celebration of Christmas. Numerous Americans place Christmas trees in their homes without subscribing to Christian religious beliefs, and when the city's tree stands alone in front of the City-County Building, it is not considered an endorsement of Christian faith. Indeed, a 40-foot Christmas tree was one of the objects that validated the creche in *Lynch*. The widely accepted view of the Christmas tree as the preeminent secular symbol of the Christmas holiday season serves to emphasize the secular component of the message communicated by other elements of an accompanying holiday display, including the Chanukah menorah.

The tree, moreover, is clearly the predominant element in the city's display. The 45-foot tree occupies the central position beneath the middle archway in front of the Grant Street entrance to the City-County Building; the 18-foot menorah is positioned to one side. Given this configuration, it is much more sensible to interpret the meaning of the menorah in light of the tree, rather than vice-versa. In the shadow of the tree, the menorah is readily understood as simply a recognition that Christmas is not the only traditional way of observing the winter holiday season. In these circumstances, then, the combination of the tree and the menorah communicates not a simultaneous endorsement of both the Christian and Jewish faiths, but instead, a secular celebration of Christmas coupled with an acknowledgment of Chanukah as a contemporaneous alternative tradition.

Although the city has used a symbol with religious meaning as its representation of Chanukah, this is not a case in which the city has reasonable alternatives that are less religious in nature. It is difficult to imagine a predominantly secular symbol of Chanukah that the city could place next to its Christmas tree. An 18-foot dreidel would look out of place, and might be interpreted by some as mocking the celebration of Chanukah. The absence of a more secular alternative symbol is itself part of the context in which the city's actions must be judged in determining the likely effect of its use of the menorah. Where the government's secular message can be conveyed by two symbols, only one of which carries religious meaning, an observer reasonably might infer from the fact that the government has chosen to use the religious symbol that the government means to promote religious faith.

But where, as here, no such choice has been made, this inference of endorsement is not present. The mayor's sign further diminishes the possibility that the tree and the menorah will be interpreted as a dual endorsement of Christianity and Judaism. The sign states that, during the holiday season, the city salutes liberty. . . . Here, the mayor's sign serves to confirm what the context already reveals: that the display of the menorah is not an endorsement of religious faith, but simply a recognition of cultural diversity. . . .

The conclusion here that, in this particular context, the menorah's display does not have an effect of endorsing religious faith does not foreclose the possibility that the display of the menorah might violate either the "purpose" or "entanglement" prong of the *Lemon* analysis. These issues were not addressed by the Court of Appeals, and may be considered by that court on remand.

VII

Lynch v. Donnelly confirms, and in no way repudiates, the longstanding constitutional principle that government may not engage in a practice that has the effect of promoting or endorsing religious beliefs. The display of the creche in the county courthouse has this unconstitutional effect. The display of the menorah in front of the City-County Building, however, does not have this effect, given its "particular physical setting."

The judgment of the Court of Appeals is affirmed in part and reversed in part, and the cases are remanded for further proceedings.

It is so ordered.

Town of
Greece v. Galloway (2014)

> *This case illustrates a shift in the Court's focus away from the concern about "endorsement" to a concern about "coercion," a shift that began in* Lee v. Weisman *in 1992. Justice Kennedy here emphasizes the unconstitutionality of forcing, or coercing, citizens into participating in religious messages. In allowing a prayer before a governmental meeting, Kennedy is signaling that some religious messages in public life—those deemed noncoercive—are acceptable.*

JUSTICE ANTHONY KENNEDY delivered the opinion of the Court.

The Court must decide whether the town of Greece, New York, imposes an impermissible establishment of religion by opening its monthly board meetings with a prayer. It must be concluded . . . that no violation of the Constitution has been shown.

I

Greece, a town with a population of 94,000, is in upstate New York. For some years, it began its monthly town board meetings with a moment of silence. In 1999, the newly elected town supervisor, John Auberger, decided to replicate the prayer practice he had found meaningful while serving in the county legislature. Following the roll call and recitation of the Pledge of Allegiance, Auberger would invite a local clergyman to the front of the room to deliver an invocation. After the prayer, Auberger would thank the minister for serving as the board's "chaplain for the month" and present him with a commemorative plaque. The prayer was intended to place town board members in a solemn and deliberative frame of mind, invoke divine guidance in town affairs, and follow a tradition practiced by Congress and dozens of state legislatures.

The town followed an informal method for selecting prayer givers, all of whom were unpaid volunteers. . . . Its leaders maintained that a minister or layperson of any persuasion, including an atheist, could give the invocation. But nearly all of the congregations in town were Christian; and from 1999 to 2007, all of the participating ministers were too.

Greece neither reviewed the prayers in advance of the meetings nor provided guidance as to their tone or content, in the belief that exercising any degree of control over the prayers would infringe both the free exercise and speech rights of the ministers. The town instead left the guest clergy free to compose their own devotions. The resulting prayers often sounded both civic and religious themes. . . .

Some of the ministers spoke in a distinctly Christian

idiom; and a minority invoked religious holidays, scripture, or doctrine. . . .

Respondents Susan Galloway and Linda Stephens attended town board meetings to speak about issues of local concern, and they objected that the prayers violated their religious or philosophical views. . . . After respondents complained that Christian themes pervaded the prayers, to the exclusion of citizens who did not share those beliefs, the town invited a Jewish layman and the chairman of the local Baha'i temple to deliver prayers. A Wiccan priestess who had read press reports about the prayer controversy requested, and was granted, an opportunity to give the invocation.

Galloway and Stephens . . . alleged that the town violated the First Amendment's Establishment Clause by preferring Christians over other prayer givers and by sponsoring sectarian prayers, such as those given "in Jesus' name." They did not seek an end to the prayer practice, but rather requested an injunction that would limit the town to "inclusive and ecumenical" prayers that referred only to a "generic God" and would not associate the government with any one faith or belief. . . .

II

. . . The Congress that drafted the First Amendment would have been accustomed to invocations containing explicitly religious themes of the sort respondents find objectionable. One of the Senate's first chaplains, the Rev. William White, gave prayers in a series that included the Lord's Prayer, the Collect for Ash Wednesday, prayers for peace and grace, a general thanksgiving, St. Chrysostom's Prayer, and a prayer seeking "the grace of our Lord Jesus Christ, &c." The decidedly Christian nature of these prayers must not be dismissed as the relic of a time when our Nation was less pluralistic than it is today. Congress continues to permit its appointed and visiting chaplains to express themselves in a religious idiom. It acknowledges our growing diversity not by proscribing sectarian content but by welcoming ministers of many creeds.

The contention that legislative prayer must be generic or nonsectarian derives from dictum in County of Allegheny that was disputed when written and has been repudiated by later cases. There the Court held that a creche placed on the steps of a county courthouse to celebrate the Christmas season violated the Establishment Clause because it had "the effect of endorsing a patently Christian message." Four dissenting Justices disputed that endorsement could be the proper test, as it likely would condemn a host of traditional practices that recognize the role religion plays in our society, among them legislative prayer and the "forthrightly religious" Thanksgiving proclamations issued by nearly every President since Washington. . . .

To hold that invocations must be nonsectarian would force the legislatures that sponsor prayers and the courts that are asked to decide these cases to act as supervisors and censors of religious speech, a rule that would involve government in religious matters to a far greater degree than is the case under the town's current practice of neither editing or approving prayers in advance nor criticizing their content after the fact. Our Government is prohibited from prescribing prayers to be recited in our public institutions in order to promote a preferred system of belief or code of moral behavior. It would be but a few steps removed from that prohibition for legislatures to require chaplains to redact the religious content from their message in order to make it acceptable for the public sphere. Government may not mandate a civic religion that stifles any but the most generic reference to the sacred any more than it may prescribe a religious orthodoxy.

Respondents argue, in effect, that legislative prayer may be addressed only to a generic God. The law and the Court could not draw this line for each specific prayer or seek to require ministers to set aside their nuanced and deeply personal beliefs for vague and artificial ones. There is doubt, in any event, that consensus might be reached as to what qualifies as generic or nonsectarian. . . . Because it is unlikely that prayer will be inclusive beyond dispute, it would be unwise to adopt what respondents think is the next-best option: permitting those religious words, and only those words, that are acceptable to the majority, even if they will exclude some. The First Amendment is not a majority rule, and government may not seek to define permissible categories of religious speech. Once it invites prayer into the public sphere, government must permit a prayer giver to address his or her own God or gods as conscience dictates, unfettered by what an administrator or judge considers to be nonsectarian.

In rejecting the suggestion that legislative prayer must be nonsectarian, the Court does not imply that no constraints remain on its content. The relevant constraint derives from its place at the opening of legislative sessions, where it is meant to lend gravity to the occasion and reflect values long part of the Nation's heritage. Prayer that is solemn and respectful in tone, that invites lawmakers to reflect upon shared ideals and common ends before they embark on the fractious business of governing, serves that legitimate function. If the course and practice over time shows that the invocations denigrate nonbelievers or religious minorities, threaten damnation, or preach conversion, many present may consider the prayer to fall short of the desire to elevate the purpose of the occasion and to unite lawmakers in their common effort. That circumstance would present a different case than the one presently before the Court. . . .

. . . [C]eremonial prayers strive for the idea that people of many faiths may be united in a community of tolerance and devotion. Even those who disagree as to religious doctrine may find common ground in the desire to show respect for the divine in all aspects of their lives and being. Our tradition assumes that adult citizens, firm in their own beliefs, can tolerate and perhaps appreciate a ceremonial prayer delivered by a person of a different faith.

The prayers delivered in the town of Greece do not fall outside the tradition this Court has recognized. A number of the prayers did invoke the name of Jesus, the Heavenly Father, or the Holy Spirit, but they also invoked universal themes, as by celebrating the changing of the seasons or calling for a "spirit of cooperation" among town leaders. . . .

Finally, the Court disagrees with the view taken by the Court of Appeals that the town of Greece contravened the Establishment Clause by inviting a predominantly Christian set of ministers to lead the prayer. The town made reasonable efforts to identify all of the congregations located within its borders and represented that it would welcome a prayer by any minister or layman who wished to give one. That nearly all of the congregations in town turned out to be Christian does not reflect an aversion or bias on the part of town leaders against minority faiths. So long as the town maintains a policy of nondiscrimination, the Constitution does not require it to search beyond its borders for non-Christian prayer givers in an effort to achieve religious balancing. The quest to promote "a 'diversity' of religious views" would require the town "to make wholly inappropriate judgments about the number of religions [it] should sponsor and the relative frequency with which it should sponsor each," a form of government entanglement with religion that is far more troublesome than the current approach.

B

Respondents . . . contend that prayer conducted in the intimate setting of a town board meeting differs in fundamental ways from the invocations delivered in Congress and state legislatures, where the public remains segregated from legislative activity and may not address the body except by occasional invitation. Citizens attend town meetings, on the other hand, to accept awards; speak on matters of local importance; and petition the board for action that may affect their economic interests, such as the granting of permits, business licenses, and zoning variances. Respondents argue that the public may feel subtle pressure to participate in prayers that violate their beliefs in order to please the board members from whom they are about to seek a favorable ruling. In their view the fact that board members in small towns know many of their constituents by name only increases the pressure to conform.

It is an elemental First Amendment principle that government may not coerce its citizens "to support or participate in any religion or its exercise." On the record in this case the Court is not persuaded that the town of Greece, through the act of offering a brief, solemn, and respectful prayer to open its monthly meetings, compelled its citizens to engage in a religious observance. . . .

The prayer opportunity in this case must be evaluated against the backdrop of historical practice. As a practice that has long endured, legislative prayer has become part of our heritage and tradition, part of our expressive idiom, similar to the Pledge of Allegiance, inaugural prayer, or the recitation of "God save the United States and this honorable

Court" at the opening of this Court's sessions. It is presumed that the reasonable observer is acquainted with this tradition and understands that its purposes are to lend gravity to public proceedings and to acknowledge the place religion holds in the lives of many private citizens, not to afford government an opportunity to proselytize or force truant constituents into the pews. That many appreciate these acknowledgments of the divine in our public institutions does not suggest that those who disagree are compelled to join the expression or approve its content.

The principal audience for these invocations is not, indeed, the public but lawmakers themselves, who may find that a moment of prayer or quiet reflection sets the mind to a higher purpose and thereby eases the task of governing. . . . To be sure, many members of the public find these prayers meaningful and wish to join them. But their purpose is largely to accommodate the spiritual needs of lawmakers and connect them to a tradition dating to the time of the Framers. For members of town boards and commissions, who often serve part-time and as volunteers, ceremonial prayer may also reflect the values they hold as private citizens. The prayer is an opportunity for them to show who and what they are without denying the right to dissent by those who disagree.

The analysis would be different if town board members directed the public to participate in the prayers, singled out dissidents for opprobrium, or indicated that their decisions might be influenced by a person's acquiescence in the prayer opportunity. No such thing occurred in the town of Greece. . . . Respondents suggest that constituents might feel pressure to join the prayers to avoid irritating the officials who would be ruling on their petitions, but this argument has no evidentiary support. . . .

In their declarations in the trial court, respondents stated that the prayers gave them offense and made them feel excluded and disrespected. Offense, however, does not equate to coercion. Adults often encounter speech they find disagreeable; and an Establishment Clause violation is not made out any time a person experiences a sense of affront from the expression of contrary religious views in a legislative forum, especially where, as here, any member of the public is welcome in turn to offer an invocation reflecting his or her own convictions. . . . But in the general course legislative bodies do not engage in impermissible coercion merely by exposing constituents to prayer they would rather not hear and in which they need not participate. . . .

In the town of Greece, the prayer is delivered during the ceremonial portion of the town's meeting. . . .

Ceremonial prayer is but a recognition that, since this Nation was founded and until the present day, many Americans deem that their own existence must be understood by precepts far beyond the authority of government to alter or define and that willing participation in civic affairs can be consistent with a brief acknowledgment of their belief in a higher power, always with due respect for those who adhere to other beliefs. The prayer in this case has a permissible ceremonial purpose. It is not an unconstitutional establishment of religion.

⸻

The town of Greece does not violate the First Amendment by opening its meetings with prayer that comports with our tradition and does not coerce participation by nonadherents. The judgment of the U.S. Court of Appeals for the Second Circuit is reversed.

It is so ordered.

American Legion v. American Humanist Association (2019)

> *In this case, the Court upheld the constitutionality of the Bladensburg Peace Cross, located in a park in Maryland. This case pushed back against both the idea of endorsement and the* Lemon *test. Instead, the Court opted for a standard that was quite permissive of religious symbols.*

Justice Alito announced the judgment of the Court.

Since 1925, the Bladensburg Peace Cross (Cross) has stood as a tribute to 49 area soldiers who gave their lives in the First World War. Eighty-nine years after the dedication of the Cross, respondents filed this lawsuit, claiming that they are offended by the sight of the memorial on public land and that its presence there and the expenditure of public funds to maintain it violate the Establishment Clause of the First Amendment. To remedy this violation, they asked a federal court to order the relocation or demolition of the Cross or at least the removal of its arms. The Court of Appeals for the Fourth Circuit agreed that the memorial is unconstitutional and remanded for a determination of the proper remedy. We now reverse.

Although the cross has long been a preeminent Christian symbol, its use in the Bladensburg memorial has a special significance. After the First World War, the picture of row after row of plain white crosses marking the overseas graves of soldiers who had lost their lives in that horrible conflict was emblazoned on the minds of Americans at home, and the adoption of the cross as the Bladensburg memorial must be viewed in that historical context. For nearly a century, the Bladensburg Cross has expressed the community's grief at the loss of the young men who perished, its thanks for their sacrifice, and its dedication to the ideals for which they fought. It has become a prominent community landmark, and its removal or radical alteration at this date would be seen by many not as a neutral act but as the manifestation of "a hostility toward religion that has no place in our Establishment Clause traditions." And contrary to respondents' intimations, there is no evidence of discriminatory intent in the selection of the design of the memorial or the decision of a Maryland commission to maintain it. The Religion Clauses of the Constitution aim to foster a society in which people of all beliefs can live together harmoniously, and the presence of the Bladensburg Cross on the land where it has stood for so many years is fully consistent with that aim.

I

A

The cross came into widespread use as a symbol of Christianity by the fourth century, and it retains that meaning today. But there are many contexts in which the symbol has also taken on a secular meaning. Indeed, there are instances in which its message is now almost entirely secular. . . .

The image used in the Bladensburg memorial—a plain Latin cross—also took on new meaning after World War I. "During and immediately after the war, the army marked soldiers' graves with temporary wooden crosses or Stars of David"—a departure from the prior practice of marking graves in American military cemeteries with uniform rectangular slabs. The vast majority of these grave markers consisted of crosses, and thus when Americans saw photographs of these cemeteries, what struck them were rows and rows of plain white crosses. As a result, the image of a simple white cross "developed into a 'central symbol'" of the conflict. . . .

. . . The image of "the crosses, row on row," stuck in people's minds, and even today for those who view World War I cemeteries in Europe, the image is arresting. . . .

B

Recognition of the cross's symbolism extended to local communities across the country. In late 1918, residents of Prince George's County, Maryland, formed a committee for the purpose of erecting a memorial for the county's fallen soldiers. . . . Although we do not know precisely why the committee chose the cross, it is unsurprising that the committee— and many others commemorating World War I—adopted a symbol so widely associated with that wrenching event. . . .

The Cross was to stand at the terminus of another World War I memorial—the National Defense Highway, which connects Washington to Annapolis. . . .

The completed monument is a 32-foot tall Latin cross that sits on a large pedestal. The American Legion's emblem is displayed at its center, and the words "Valor," "Endurance," "Courage," and "Devotion" are inscribed at its base, one on each of the four faces. The pedestal also features a 9- by 2.5-foot bronze plaque explaining that the monument is "Dedicated to the heroes of Prince George's County, Maryland who lost their lives in the Great War for the liberty of the world." The plaque lists the names of 49 local men, both Black and White, who died in the war. It identifies the dates of American involvement, and quotes President Woodrow Wilson's request for a declaration of war: "The right is more precious than peace. We shall fight for the things we have always carried nearest our hearts. To such a task we dedicate our lives." . . .

C

In 2012, nearly 90 years after the Cross was dedicated and more than 50 years after the Commission acquired it, the American Humanist Association (AHA) lodged a complaint with the Commission. The complaint alleged that the Cross's presence on public land and the Commission's maintenance of the memorial violate the Establishment Clause of the First Amendment. The AHA, along with three residents of Washington, D.C., and Maryland, also sued the Commission in the District Court for the District of Maryland, making the same claim. . . . The American Legion intervened to defend the Cross. . . .

II

A

The Establishment Clause of the First Amendment provides that "Congress shall make no law respecting an establishment of religion." While the concept of a formally established church is straightforward, pinning down the meaning of a "law respecting an establishment of religion" has proved to be a vexing problem. . . . After grappling with such cases for more than 20 years, *Lemon* ambitiously attempted to distill from the Court's existing case law a test that would bring order and predictability to Establishment Clause decision making. That test, as noted, called on courts to examine the purposes and effects of a challenged government action, as well as any entanglement with religion that it might entail. . . .

If the *Lemon* Court thought that its test would provide a framework for all future Establishment Clause decisions, its expectation has not been met. In many cases, this Court has either expressly declined to apply the test or has simply ignored it.

This pattern is a testament to the *Lemon* test's shortcomings. As Establishment Clause cases involving a great array of laws and practices came to the Court, it became more and more apparent that the *Lemon* test could not resolve them. . . .

For at least four reasons, the *Lemon* test presents particularly daunting problems in cases, including the one now before us, that involve the use, for ceremonial, celebratory, or commemorative purposes, of words or symbols with religious associations. Together, these considerations counsel against efforts to evaluate such cases under *Lemon* and toward application of a presumption of constitutionality for long-standing monuments, symbols, and practices.

B

First, these cases often concern monuments, symbols, or practices that were first established long ago, and in such cases, identifying their original purpose or purposes may be especially difficult. . . .

Second, as time goes by, the purposes associated with an established monument, symbol, or practice often multiply. . . .

The existence of multiple purposes is not exclusive to longstanding monuments, symbols, or practices, but this phenomenon is more likely to occur in such cases. Even if the original purpose of a monument was infused with religion, the passage of time may obscure that sentiment. As our society becomes more and more religiously diverse, a community may preserve such monuments, symbols, and practices for the sake of their historical significance or their place in a common cultural heritage. . . .

Third, just as the purpose for maintaining a monument, symbol, or practice may evolve, "[t]he 'message' conveyed . . . may change over time." Consider, for example, the message of the Statue of Liberty, which began as a monument to the solidarity and friendship between France and the United States and only decades later came to be seen "as a beacon welcoming immigrants to a land of freedom."

With sufficient time, religiously expressive monuments, symbols, and practices can become embedded features of a community's landscape and identity. The community may come to value them without necessarily embracing their religious roots. The recent tragic fire at Notre Dame in Paris provides a striking example. Although the French Republic rigorously enforces a secular public square, the cathedral remains a symbol of national importance to the religious and nonreligious alike. Notre Dame is fundamentally a place of worship and retains great religious importance, but its meaning has broadened. For many, it is inextricably linked with the very idea of Paris and France. . . .

In the same way, consider the many cities and towns across the United States that bear religious names. Religion undoubtedly motivated those who named Bethlehem, Pennsylvania; Las Cruces, New Mexico; Providence, Rhode Island; Corpus Christi, Texas; Nephi, Utah, and the countless other places in our country with names that are rooted in religion. Yet few would argue that this history requires that these names be erased from the map. . . .

Fourth, when time's passage imbues a religiously expressive monument, symbol, or practice with this kind of familiarity and historical significance, removing it may no longer appear neutral, especially to the local community for which it has taken on particular meaning. A government that roams the land, tearing down monuments with religious symbolism and scrubbing away any reference to the divine will strike many as aggressively hostile to religion. . . .

These four considerations show that retaining established, religiously expressive monuments, symbols, and practices is quite different from erecting or adopting new ones. The passage of time gives rise to a strong presumption of constitutionality.

C

The role of the cross in World War I memorials is illustrative of each of the four preceding considerations. . . . The solemn image of endless rows of white crosses became inextricably linked with and symbolic of the ultimate price paid by 116,000 soldiers. And this relationship between the cross and the war undoubtedly influenced the design of the many war memorials that sprang up across the Nation.

This is not to say that the cross's association with the war was the sole or dominant motivation for the inclusion of the symbol in every World War I memorial that features it. But today, it is all but impossible to tell whether that was so. The passage of time means that testimony from those actually involved in the decision making process is generally unavailable, and attempting to uncover their motivations invites rampant speculation. And no matter what the original purposes for the erection of a monument, a community may wish to preserve it for very different reasons, such as the historic preservation and traffic-safety concerns the Commission has pressed here. . . .

III

Applying these principles, we conclude that the Bladensburg Cross does not violate the Establishment Clause.

As we have explained, the Bladensburg Cross carries special significance in commemorating World War I. Due in large part to the image of the simple wooden crosses that originally marked the graves of American soldiers killed in the war, the cross became a symbol of their sacrifice, and the design of the Bladensburg Cross must be understood in light of that background. That the cross originated as a Christian symbol and retains that meaning in many contexts does not change the fact that the symbol took on an added secular meaning when used in World War I memorials.

Not only did the Bladensburg Cross begin with this meaning, but with the passage of time, it has acquired historical importance. It reminds the people of Bladensburg and surrounding areas of the deeds of their predecessors and of the sacrifices they made in a war fought in the name of democracy. As long as it is retained in its original place and form, it speaks as well of the community that erected the monument nearly a century ago and has maintained it ever since. The memorial represents what the relatives, friends, and neighbors of the fallen soldiers felt at the time and how they chose to express their sentiments. And the monument has acquired additional layers of historical meaning in subsequent years. The Cross now stands among memorials to veterans of later wars. It has become part of the community.

The monument would not serve that role if its design had deliberately disrespected area soldiers who perished in World War I. More than 3,500 Jewish soldiers gave their lives for the United States in that conflict, and some have wondered whether the names of any Jewish soldiers from the area were deliberately left off the list on the memorial or whether the names of any Jewish soldiers were included on the Cross against the wishes of their families. There is no evidence that either thing was done, and we do know that one of the local American Legion leaders responsible for the Cross's construction was a Jewish veteran.

The AHA's brief strains to connect the Bladensburg Cross and even the American Legion with anti-Semitism and the Ku Klux Klan, but the AHA's disparaging intimations have no evidentiary support. And when the events surrounding the erection of the Cross are viewed in historical context, a very different picture may perhaps be discerned. The monument was dedicated on July 12, 1925, during a period when the country was experiencing heightened racial and religious animosity. Membership in the Ku Klux Klan, which preached hatred of Blacks, Catholics, and Jews, was at its height. On August 8, 1925, just two weeks after the dedication of the Bladensburg Cross and less than 10 miles away, some 30,000 robed Klansmen marched down Pennsylvania Avenue in the Nation's Capital. But the Bladensburg Cross memorial included the names of both Black and White soldiers who had given their lives in the war; and despite the fact that Catholics and Baptists at that time were not exactly in the habit of participating together in ecumenical services, the ceremony dedicating the Cross began with an invocation by a Catholic priest and ended with a benediction by a Baptist pastor. We can never know for certain what was in the minds of those responsible for the memorial, but in light of what we know about this ceremony, we can perhaps make out a picture of a community that, at least for the moment, was united by grief and patriotism and rose above the divisions of the day.

Finally, it is surely relevant that the monument commemorates the death of particular individuals. It is natural and appropriate for those seeking to honor the deceased to invoke the symbols that signify what death meant for those who are memorialized. In some circumstances, the exclusion of any such recognition would make a memorial incomplete. This well explains why Holocaust memorials invariably include Stars of David or other symbols of Judaism. It explains why a new memorial to Native American veterans in Washington, D.C., will portray a steel circle to represent "'the hole in the sky where the creator lives.'" And this is why the memorial for soldiers from the Bladensburg community features the cross—the same symbol that marks the graves of so many of their comrades near the battlefields where they fell.

IV

The cross is undoubtedly a Christian symbol, but that fact should not blind us to everything else that the Bladensburg Cross has come to represent. For some, that monument is a symbolic resting place for ancestors who never returned home. For others, it is a place for the community to gather and honor all veterans and their sacrifices for our Nation. For others still, it is a historical landmark. For many of these people, destroying or defacing the Cross that has stood undisturbed for nearly a century would not be neutral and would not further the ideals of respect and tolerance embodied in the First Amendment. For all these reasons, the Cross does not offend the Constitution.

———

We reverse the judgment of the Court of Appeals for the Fourth Circuit and remand the cases for further proceedings.

It is so ordered.

Part III

THE RIGHT
to
PRACTICE RELIGION

Sherbert v. Verner (1963)

*In this section, we examine cases in which religious peo-
ple have argued that the government has limited their
religious freedom. As this case demonstrates, the Court was
previously very protective of that freedom, finding that
even unintentional limits on religious beliefs and practices
could violate the Free Exercise Clause. In cases like this,
even though the law in question could remain valid, individuals with religious reasons for not following the law did
not have to comply with it and were entitled to exemptions.* Sherbert v. Verner *concerns a woman denied unemployment assistance after she was fired from her job for
insisting that she take Saturday rather than Sunday off, in
accordance with her religious beliefs.*

MR. JUSTICE BRENNAN delivered the opinion of the
Court.

Appellant, a member of the Seventh-day Adventist
Church, was discharged by her South Carolina employer because she would not work on Saturday, the Sabbath Day of
her faith. When she was unable to obtain other employment
because, from conscientious scruples, she would not take

Saturday work, she filed a claim for unemployment compensation benefits under the South Carolina Unemployment Compensation Act. That law provides that, to be eligible for benefits, a claimant must be "able to work and . . . available for work"; and, further, that a claimant is ineligible for benefits "[i]f . . . he has failed, without good cause . . . to accept available suitable work when offered him by the employment office or the employer. . . ."

The appellee Employment Security Commission, in administrative proceedings under the statute, found that appellant's restriction upon her availability for Saturday work brought her within the provision disqualifying for benefits insured workers who fail, without good cause, to accept "suitable work when offered . . . by the employment office or the employer. . . ." The Commission's finding was sustained by the Court of Common Pleas for Spartanburg County. That court's judgment was, in turn, affirmed by the South Carolina Supreme Court, which rejected appellant's contention that, as applied to her, the disqualifying provisions of the South Carolina statute abridged her right to the free exercise of her religion secured under the Free Exercise Clause of the First Amendment through the Fourteenth Amendment. The State Supreme Court held specifically that appellant's ineligibility infringed no constitutional liberties because such a construction of the statute "places no restriction upon the appellant's freedom of religion, nor does it in any way prevent her in the exercise of her right and freedom to observe her religious beliefs in accordance with the dictates of her conscience."

We noted probable jurisdiction of appellant's appeal. We reverse the judgment of the South Carolina Supreme Court and remand for further proceedings not inconsistent with this opinion.

I

The door of the Free Exercise Clause stands tightly closed against any governmental regulation of religious beliefs as such. Government may neither compel affirmation of a repugnant belief, nor penalize or discriminate against individuals or groups because they hold religious views abhorrent to the authorities, nor employ the taxing power to inhibit the dissemination of particular religious views. On the other hand, the Court has rejected challenges under the Free Exercise Clause to governmental regulation of certain overt acts prompted by religious beliefs or principles, for "even when the action is in accord with one's religious convictions, [it] is not totally free from legislative restrictions." The conduct or actions so regulated have invariably posed some substantial threat to public safety, peace or order.

Plainly enough, appellant's conscientious objection to Saturday work constitutes no conduct prompted by religious principles of a kind within the reach of state legislation. If, therefore, the decision of the South Carolina Supreme Court is to withstand appellant's constitutional challenge, it must be either because her disqualification as a beneficiary represents no infringement by the State of her constitutional rights of free exercise, or because any incidental burden on the free exercise of appellant's religion may be justified by a "compelling state interest in the regulation of a subject within the State's constitutional power to regulate. . . ."

II

We turn first to the question whether the disqualification for benefits imposes any burden on the free exercise of appellant's religion. We think it is clear that it does. In a sense, the consequences of such a disqualification to religious principles and practices may be only an indirect result of welfare legislation within the State's general competence to enact; it is true that no criminal sanctions directly compel appellant to work a six-day week. But this is only the beginning, not the end, of our inquiry.

Here, not only is it apparent that appellant's declared ineligibility for benefits derives solely from the practice of her religion, but the pressure upon her to forego that practice is unmistakable. The ruling forces her to choose between following the precepts of her religion and forfeiting benefits, on the one hand, and abandoning one of the precepts of her religion in order to accept work, on the other hand. Governmental imposition of such a choice puts the same kind of burden upon the free exercise of religion as would a fine imposed against appellant for her Saturday worship.

Nor may the South Carolina court's construction of the statute be saved from constitutional infirmity on the ground that unemployment compensation benefits are not appellant's "right," but merely a "privilege." It is too late in the day to doubt that the liberties of religion and expression may be infringed by the denial of or placing of conditions upon a benefit or privilege. . . .

In *Speiser v. Randall*, we emphasized that conditions upon public benefits cannot be sustained if they so operate, whatever their purpose, to inhibit or deter the exercise of First

Amendment freedoms. We there struck down a condition which limited the availability of a tax exemption to those members of the exempted class who affirmed their loyalty to the state government granting the exemption. While the State was surely under no obligation to afford such an exemption, we held that the imposition of such a condition upon even a gratuitous benefit inevitably deterred or discouraged the exercise of First Amendment rights of expression, and thereby threatened to "produce a result which the State could not command directly." . . . Likewise, to condition the availability of benefits upon this appellant's willingness to violate a cardinal principle of her religious faith effectively penalizes the free exercise of her constitutional liberties.

Significantly, South Carolina expressly saves the Sunday worshipper from having to make the kind of choice which we here hold infringes the Sabbatarian's religious liberty. When, in times of "national emergency," the textile plants are authorized by the State Commissioner of Labor to operate on Sunday, "no employee shall be required to work on Sunday . . . who is conscientiously opposed to Sunday work, and if any employee should refuse to work on Sunday on account of conscientious . . . objections, he or she shall not jeopardize his or her seniority by such refusal or be discriminated against in any other manner."

No question of the disqualification of a Sunday worshipper for benefits is likely to arise, since we cannot suppose that an employer will discharge him in violation of this statute. The unconstitutionality of the disqualification of the Sabbatarian is thus compounded by the religious discrimination which South Carolina's general statutory scheme necessarily effects.

III

We must next consider whether some compelling state interest enforced in the eligibility provisions of the South Carolina statute justifies the substantial infringement of appellant's First Amendment right. It is basic that no showing merely of a rational relationship to some colorable state interest would suffice; in this highly sensitive constitutional area, "[o]nly the gravest abuses, endangering paramount interests, give occasion for permissible limitation."

No such abuse or danger has been advanced in the present case. The appellees suggest no more than a possibility that the filing of fraudulent claims by unscrupulous claimants feigning religious objections to Saturday work might not only dilute the unemployment compensation fund, but also hinder the scheduling by employers of necessary Saturday work. But that possibility is not apposite here, because no such objection appears to have been made before the South Carolina Supreme Court, and we are unwilling to assess the importance of an asserted state interest without the views of the state court. Nor, if the contention had been made below, would the record appear to sustain it; there is no proof whatever to warrant such fears of malingering or deceit as those which the respondents now advance. Even if consideration of such evidence is not foreclosed by the prohibition against judicial inquiry into the truth or falsity of religious beliefs, *United States v. Ballard*—a question as to which we intimate no view, since it is not before us—it is highly doubtful whether such evidence would be sufficient to warrant a substantial infringement of religious liberties. For even if the possibility of spurious claims did threaten to dilute the fund and disrupt the scheduling of work, it would plainly be incumbent upon the appellees to demonstrate that no alternative forms of regulation would combat such abuses without infringing First Amendment rights.

In these respects, then, the state interest asserted in the present case is wholly dissimilar to the interests which were found to justify the less direct burden upon religious practices in *Braunfeld v. Brown.* The Court recognized that the Sunday closing law which that decision sustained undoubtedly served "to make the practice of [the Orthodox Jewish merchants'] . . . religious beliefs more expensive." But the statute was nevertheless saved by a countervailing factor which finds no equivalent in the instant case—a strong state interest in providing one uniform day of rest for all workers. That secular objective could be achieved, the Court found, only by declaring Sunday to be that day of rest. Requiring exemptions for Sabbatarians, while theoretically possible, appeared to present an administrative problem of such magnitude, or to afford the exempted class so great a competitive advantage, that such a requirement would have rendered the entire statutory scheme unworkable. In the present case, no such justifications underlie the determination of the state court that appellant's religion makes her ineligible to receive benefits.

IV

In holding as we do, plainly we are not fostering the "establishment" of the Seventh-day Adventist religion in South Carolina, for the extension of unemployment benefits to Sabbatarians in common with Sunday worshippers reflects nothing more than the governmental obligation of neutrality in the face of religious differences, and does not represent that involvement of religious with secular institutions which it is the object of the Establishment Clause to forestall. Nor does the recognition of the appellant's right to unemployment benefits under the state statute serve to abridge any other person's religious liberties. Nor do we, by our decision today, declare the existence of a constitutional right to unemployment benefits on the part of all persons whose religious convictions are the cause of their unemployment. This is not a case in which an employee's religious convictions serve to make him a nonproductive member of society. Finally, nothing we say today constrains the States to adopt any particular form or scheme of unemployment compensation. Our holding today is only that South Carolina may not constitutionally apply the eligibility provisions so as to constrain a worker to abandon his religious convictions respecting the day of rest. . . .

In view of the result we have reached under the First and Fourteenth Amendments' guarantee of free exercise of religion, we have no occasion to consider appellant's claim that the denial of benefits also deprived her of the equal protection of the laws in violation of the Fourteenth Amendment.

The judgment of the South Carolina Supreme Court is reversed, and the case is remanded for further proceedings not inconsistent with this opinion.

It is so ordered.

Employment Division v. Smith (1990)

> *While Ms. Sherbert won her case in the excerpt above, over time the Court became less willing to grant religious exemptions from general laws. Here, Justice Antonin Scalia denies an exemption to two Native Americans who had been rejected for unemployment compensation after having been fired for their use of peyote—which was banned in the state—in a religious ceremony. The case is significant because it stands for a more general shift in the Court's approach to religious freedom, away from considering the effects of laws on religious belief, and toward an inquiry about intentional or explicit discrimination by government against religious believers.*

Justice SCALIA delivered the opinion of the Court.

This case requires us to decide whether the Free Exercise Clause of the First Amendment permits the State of Oregon to include religiously inspired peyote use within the reach of its general criminal prohibition on use of that drug, and thus permits the State to deny unemployment benefits to persons dismissed from their jobs because of such religiously inspired use.

I

Oregon law prohibits the knowing or intentional possession of a "controlled substance" unless the substance has been prescribed by a medical practitioner. The law defines "controlled substance" as a drug classified in Schedules I through V of the Federal Controlled Substances Act. Persons who violate this provision by possessing a controlled substance listed on Schedule I are "guilty of a Class B felony." . . . Schedule I contains the drug peyote, a hallucinogen derived from the plant Lophophora williamsii Lemaire.

Respondents Alfred Smith and Galen Black were fired from their jobs with a private drug rehabilitation organization because they ingested peyote for sacramental purposes at a ceremony of the Native American Church, of which both are members. When respondents applied to petitioner Employment Division for unemployment compensation, they were determined to be ineligible for benefits because they had been discharged for work-related "misconduct". The Oregon Court of Appeals reversed that determination, holding that the denial of benefits violated respondents' free exercise rights under the First Amendment. . . .

II

. . . Now that the Oregon Supreme Court has confirmed that Oregon does prohibit the religious use of peyote, we proceed to consider whether that prohibition is permissible under the Free Exercise Clause.

A

The Free Exercise Clause of the First Amendment, which has been made applicable to the States by incorporation into the Fourteenth Amendment, provides that "Congress shall make no law respecting an establishment of religion, or *prohibiting the free exercise thereof. . . .*" The free exercise of religion means, first and foremost, the right to believe and profess whatever religious doctrine one desires. Thus, the First Amendment obviously excludes all "governmental regulation of religious beliefs as such." The government may not compel affirmation of religious belief, punish the expression of religious doctrines it believes to be false, impose special disabilities on the basis of religious views or religious status, or lend its power to one or the other side in controversies over religious authority or dogma.

But the "exercise of religion" often involves not only belief and profession but the performance of (or abstention from) physical acts: assembling with others for a worship service, participating in sacramental use of bread and wine, proselytizing, abstaining from certain foods or certain modes of transportation. It would be true, we think (though no case of ours has involved the point), that a state would be "prohibiting the free exercise [of religion]" if it sought to ban such acts or abstentions only when they are engaged in for religious reasons, or only because of the religious belief that they display. It would doubtless be unconstitutional, for example, to ban the casting of "statues that are to be used for worship purposes," or to prohibit bowing down before a golden calf.

Respondents in the present case, however, seek to carry the meaning of "prohibiting the free exercise [of religion]" one large step further. They contend that their religious motivation for using peyote places them beyond the reach of a criminal law that is not specifically directed at their religious practice, and that is concededly constitutional as applied to those who use the drug for other reasons. They assert, in other words, that "prohibiting the free exercise [of religion]" includes requiring any individual to observe a generally applicable law that requires (or forbids) the performance of an act that his religious belief forbids (or requires). As a textual matter, we do not think the words must be given that meaning. . . . It is a permissible reading of the text . . . to say that, if prohibiting the exercise of religion (or burdening the activity of printing) is not the object of the tax, but merely the incidental effect of a generally applicable and otherwise valid provision, the First Amendment has not been offended. . . .

. . . We have never held that an individual's religious beliefs excuse him from compliance with an otherwise valid law prohibiting conduct that the State is free to regulate. On the contrary, the record of more than a century of our free exercise jurisprudence contradicts that proposition. . . .

We first had occasion to assert that principle in *Reynolds v. United States* (1879), where we rejected the claim that criminal laws against polygamy could not be constitutionally applied to those whose religion commanded the practice. "Laws," we said, "are made for the government of actions, and while they cannot interfere with mere religious belief and opinions, they may with practices. . . . Can a man excuse his practices to the contrary because of his religious belief? To permit this would be to make the professed doctrines of religious belief superior to the law of the land, and in effect to permit every citizen to become a law unto himself."

Subsequent decisions have consistently held that the right of free exercise does not relieve an individual of the obligation to comply with a "valid and neutral law of general applicability on the ground that the law proscribes (or prescribes) conduct that his religion prescribes (or proscribes)." . . .

The only decisions in which we have held that the First Amendment bars application of a neutral, generally applicable law to religiously motivated action have involved not the Free Exercise Clause alone, but the Free Exercise Clause in conjunction with other constitutional protections, such as freedom of speech and of the press . . . or the right of parents . . . to direct the education of their children. . . .

The present case does not present such a hybrid situation, but a free exercise claim unconnected with any communicative activity or parental right. Respondents urge us to hold, quite simply, that when otherwise prohibitable conduct is accompanied by religious convictions, not only the convictions but the conduct itself must be free from governmental regulation. We have never held that, and decline to do so now. . . .

Values that are protected against government interference through enshrinement in the Bill of Rights are not thereby banished from the political process. Just as a society that believes in the negative protection accorded to the press by the First Amendment is likely to enact laws that affirmatively foster the dissemination of the printed word, so also a society that believes in the negative protection accorded to religious belief can be expected to be solicitous of that value in its legislation as well. It is therefore not surprising that a number of States have made an exception to their drug laws for sacramental peyote use. But to say that a nondiscriminatory religious practice exemption is permitted, or even that it is desirable, is not to say that it is constitutionally required, and that the appropriate occasions for its creation can be discerned by the courts. It may fairly be said that leaving accommodation to the political process will place at a relative disadvantage those religious practices that are not widely engaged in; but that unavoidable consequence of democratic government must be preferred to a system in which each conscience is a law unto itself or in which judges weigh the social importance of all laws against the centrality of all religious beliefs.

———

Because respondents' ingestion of peyote was prohibited under Oregon law, and because that prohibition is constitutional, Oregon may, consistent with the Free Exercise Clause, deny respondents unemployment compensation when their dismissal results from use of the drug. The decision of the Oregon Supreme Court is accordingly reversed.

It is so ordered.

Church of the Lukumi Babalu Aye, Inc. v. Hialeah (1993)

> *Although after the Court's decision in* Smith *religious claimants had to meet a higher burden to win Free Exercise cases, the following case represents an instance in which claimants were still successful. In this case, the Court strikes down a law banning animal sacrifice on the grounds that it was directly intended to discriminate against a specific religious practice engaged in by members of the Church of the Lukumi Babalu Aye, thereby inhibiting their free exercise of religion.*

I

A

This case involves practices of the Santeria religion, which originated in the 19th century. When hundreds of thousands of members of the Yoruba people were brought as slaves from western Africa to Cuba, their traditional African religion absorbed significant elements of Roman Catholicism. The resulting syncretion, or fusion, is Santeria, "the way of the saints." The Cuban Yoruba express their devotion to spirits, called *orishas*, through the iconography of Catholic saints, Catholic symbols are often present at Santeria rites, and Santeria devotees attend the Catholic sacraments.

The Santeria faith teaches that every individual has a destiny from God, a destiny fulfilled with the aid and energy of the *orishas*. The basis of the Santeria religion is the nurture of a personal relation with the *orishas*, and one of the principal forms of devotion is an animal sacrifice. The sacrifice of animals as part of religious rituals has ancient roots. Animal sacrifice is mentioned throughout the Old Testament, and it played an important role in the practice of Judaism before destruction of the second Temple in Jerusalem. In modern Islam, there is an annual sacrifice commemorating Abraham's sacrifice of a ram in the stead of his son.

According to Santeria teaching, the *orishas* are powerful but not immortal. They depend for survival on the sacrifice. Sacrifices are performed at birth, marriage, and death rites, for the cure of the sick, for the initiation of new members and priests, and during an annual celebration. Animals sacrificed in Santeria rituals include chickens, pigeons, doves, ducks, guinea pigs, goats, sheep, and turtles. The animals are killed by the cutting of the carotid arteries in the neck. The sacrificed animal is cooked and eaten, except after healing and death rituals.

Santeria adherents faced widespread persecution in Cuba, so the religion and its rituals were practiced in secret. The open practice of Santeria and its rites remains infrequent. The religion was brought to this Nation most often by exiles from the Cuban revolution. The District Court estimated that there are at least 50,000 practitioners in South Florida today.

B

Petitioner Church of the Lukumi Babalu Aye, Inc. (Church), is a not-for-profit corporation organized under Florida law in 1973. The Church and its congregants practice the Santeria religion. The president of the Church is petitioner Ernesto Pichardo, who is also the Church's priest and holds the religious title of *Italero*, the second highest in the Santeria faith. In April 1987, the Church leased land in the city of Hialeah, Florida, and announced plans to establish a house of worship as well as a school, cultural center, and museum. Pichardo indicated that the Church's goal was to bring the practice of the Santeria faith, including its ritual of animal sacrifice, into the open. The Church began the process of obtaining utility service and receiving the necessary licensing, inspection, and zoning approvals. Although the Church's efforts at obtaining the necessary licenses and permits were far from smooth, it appears that it received all needed approvals by early August 1987.

The prospect of a Santeria church in their midst was distressing to many members of the Hialeah community, and the announcement of the plans to open a Santeria church in Hialeah prompted the city council to hold an emergency public session on June 9, 1987. . . .

A summary suffices here, beginning with the enactments passed at the June 9 meeting. First, the city council adopted Resolution 87-66, which noted the "concern" expressed by residents of the city "that certain religions may propose to engage in practices which are inconsistent with public morals, peace or safety," and declared that "[t]he City reiterates its commitment to a prohibition against any and all acts of any and all religious groups which are inconsistent with public morals, peace or safety." Next, the council approved an emergency ordinance, Ordinance 87-40, which incorporated in full, except as to penalty, Florida's animal cruelty laws. Among other things, the incorporated state law subjected to criminal punishment "[w]hoever . . . unnecessarily or cruelly . . . kills any animal." . . .

In September 1987, the city council adopted three substantive ordinances addressing the issue of religious animal sacrifice. Ordinance 87-52 defined "sacrifice" as "to unnecessarily kill, torment, torture, or mutilate an animal in a public or private ritual or ceremony not for the primary purpose of food consumption," and prohibited owning or possessing an animal "intending to use such animal for food purposes." It restricted application of this prohibition, however, to any individual or group that "kills, slaughters or sacrifices animals for any type of ritual, regardless of whether or not the flesh or blood of the animal is to be consumed." The ordinance contained an exemption for slaughtering by "licensed establishment[s]" of animals "specifically raised for food purposes." Declaring, moreover, that the city council "has determined that the sacrificing of animals within the city limits is contrary to the public health, safety, welfare and morals of the community," the city council adopted Ordinance 87-71. That ordinance . . . provided that "[i]t shall be unlawful for any person, persons, corporations or associations to sacrifice any animal within the corporate limits of the City of Hialeah, Florida." The final Ordinance, 87-72, defined "slaughter" as "the killing of animals for food" and prohibited slaughter outside of areas zoned for slaughterhouse use. . . . Violations of each of the four ordinances were punishable by fines not exceeding $500 or imprisonment not exceeding 60 days, or both.

Following enactment of these ordinances, the Church and

Pichardo filed this action . . . in the United States District Court for the Southern District of Florida. Named as defendants were the city of Hialeah and its mayor and members of its city council in their individual capacities. Alleging violations of petitioners' rights under the Free Exercise Clause, the complaint sought a declaratory judgment and injunctive and monetary relief. . . .

II

. . . In addressing the constitutional protection for free exercise of religion, our cases establish the general proposition that a law that is neutral and of general applicability need not be justified by a compelling governmental interest even if the law has the incidental effect of burdening a particular religious practice. Neutrality and general applicability are interrelated, and, as becomes apparent in this case, failure to satisfy one requirement is a likely indication that the other has not been satisfied. A law failing to satisfy these requirements must be justified by a compelling governmental interest and must be narrowly tailored to advance that interest. These ordinances fail to satisfy the *Smith* requirements. We begin by discussing neutrality.

A

In our Establishment Clause cases we have often stated the principle that the First Amendment forbids an official purpose to disapprove of a particular religion or of religion in general. These cases, however, for the most part have addressed governmental efforts to benefit religion or particular religions, and so have dealt with a question different, at least in its formulation and emphasis, from the issue here. Petitioners allege an attempt to disfavor their religion because of the religious ceremonies it commands, and the Free Exercise Clause is dispositive in our analysis.

At a minimum, the protections of the Free Exercise Clause pertain if the law at issue discriminates against some or all religious beliefs or regulates or prohibits conduct because it is undertaken for religious reasons. . . .

1

Although a law targeting religious beliefs as such is never permissible, if the object of a law is to infringe upon or restrict practices because of their religious motivation, the law is not neutral, and it is invalid unless it is justified by a compelling interest and is narrowly tailored to advance that interest. There are, of course, many ways of demonstrating that the object or purpose of a law is the suppression of religion or religious conduct. To determine the object of a law, we must begin with its text, for the minimum requirement of neutrality is that a law not discriminate on its face. A law lacks facial neutrality if it refers to a religious practice without a secular meaning discernible from the language or context. Petitioners contend that three of the ordinances fail this test of facial neutrality because they use the words "sacrifice" and "ritual," words with strong religious connotations. We agree that these words are consistent with the claim of facial discrimination, but the argument is not conclusive. The words "sacrifice" and "ritual" have a religious origin, but current use admits also of secular meanings. The ordinances, furthermore, define "sacrifice" in secular terms, without referring to religious practices.

We reject the contention advanced by the city that our inquiry must end with the text of the laws at issue. Facial neutrality is not determinative. The Free Exercise

Clause, like the Establishment Clause, extends beyond facial discrimination. . . .

The record in this case compels the conclusion that suppression of the central element of the Santeria worship service was the object of the ordinances. First, though use of the words "sacrifice" and "ritual" does not compel a finding of improper targeting of the Santeria religion, the choice of these words is support for our conclusion. There are further respects in which the text of the city council's enactments discloses the improper attempt to target Santeria.

Resolution 87-66, adopted June 9, 1987, recited that "residents and citizens of the City of Hialeah have expressed their concern that certain religions may propose to engage in practices which are inconsistent with public morals, peace or safety," and "reiterate[d]" the city's commitment to prohibit "any and all [such] acts of any and all religious groups." No one suggests, and on this record it cannot be maintained, that city officials had in mind a religion other than Santeria.

It becomes evident that these ordinances target Santeria sacrifice when the ordinances' operation is considered. Apart from the text, the effect of a law in its real operation is strong evidence of its object. To be sure, adverse impact will not always lead to a finding of impermissible targeting. For example, a social harm may have been a legitimate concern of government for reasons quite apart from discrimination. The subject at hand does implicate, of course, multiple concerns unrelated to religious animosity, for example, the suffering or mistreatment visited upon the sacrificed animals and health hazards from improper disposal. But the ordinances when considered together disclose an object remote from these legitimate concerns. The design of these laws accomplishes instead a "religious gerrymander," an impermissible attempt to target petitioners and their religious practices.

It is a necessary conclusion that almost the only conduct subject to Ordinances 87-40, 87-52, and 87-71 is the religious exercise of Santeria church members. The texts show that they were drafted in tandem to achieve this result. . . .

. . . The net result of the gerrymander is that few if any killings of animals are prohibited other than Santeria sacrifice, which is proscribed because it occurs during a ritual or ceremony and its primary purpose is to make an offering to the *orishas*, not food consumption. Indeed, careful drafting ensured that, although Santeria sacrifice is prohibited, killings that are no more necessary or humane in almost all other circumstances are unpunished. . . .

We also find significant evidence of the ordinances' improper targeting of Santeria sacrifice in the fact that they proscribe more religious conduct than is necessary to achieve their stated ends. . . .

2

In determining if the object of a law is a neutral one under the Free Exercise Clause, we can also find guidance in our equal protection cases. . . . Here, as in equal protection cases, we may determine the city council's object from both direct and circumstantial evidence. Relevant evidence includes, among other things, the historical background of the decision under challenge, the specific series of events leading to the enactment or official policy in question, and the legislative or administrative history, including contemporaneous statements made by members of the decisionmaking body. These objective factors bear on the question of discriminatory object.

That the ordinances were enacted "'because of,' not merely 'in spite of,'" their suppression of Santeria religious practice, is revealed by the events preceding their enactment.

Although respondent claimed at oral argument that it had experienced significant problems resulting from the sacrifice of animals within the city before the announced opening of the Church, the city council made no attempt to address the supposed problem before its meeting in June 1987, just weeks after the Church announced plans to open. The minutes and taped excerpts of the June 9 session, both of which are in the record, evidence significant hostility exhibited by residents, members of the city council, and other city officials toward the Santeria religion and its practice of animal sacrifice. The public crowd that attended the June 9 meetings interrupted statements by council members critical of Santeria with cheers and the brief comments of Pichardo with taunts. . . .

. . . This history discloses the object of the ordinances to target animal sacrifice by Santeria worshippers because of its religious motivation.

3

In sum, the neutrality inquiry leads to one conclusion: The ordinances had as their object the suppression of religion. The pattern we have recited discloses animosity to Santeria adherents and their religious practices; the ordinances by their own terms target this religious exercise; the texts of the ordinances were gerrymandered with care to proscribe religious killings of animals but to exclude almost all secular killings; and the ordinances suppress much more religious conduct than is necessary in order to achieve the legitimate ends asserted in their defense. These ordinances are not neutral, and the court below committed clear error in failing to reach this conclusion. . . .

B

The principle that government, in pursuit of legitimate interests, cannot in a selective manner impose burdens only on
conduct motivated by religious belief is essential to the protection of the rights guaranteed by the Free Exercise Clause.
The principle underlying the general applicability requirement has parallels in our First Amendment jurisprudence. In
this case we need not define with precision the standard used
to evaluate whether a prohibition is of general application, for
these ordinances fall well below the minimum standard necessary to protect First Amendment rights.

Respondent claims that Ordinances 87-40, 87-52, and
87-71 advance two interests: protecting the public health and
preventing cruelty to animals. The ordinances are underinclusive for those ends. They fail to prohibit nonreligious conduct that endangers these interests in a similar or greater
degree than Santeria sacrifice does. The underinclusion is
substantial, not inconsequential. Despite the city's proffered
interest in preventing cruelty to animals, the ordinances are
drafted with care to forbid few killings but those occasioned
by religious sacrifice. Many types of animal deaths or kills for
nonreligious reasons are either not prohibited or approved by
express provision. . . .

The ordinances are also underinclusive with regard to the
city's interest in public health, which is threatened by the disposal of animal carcasses in open public places and the consumption of uninspected meat. Neither interest is pursued by
respondent with regard to conduct that is not motivated by
religious conviction. The health risks posed by the improper
disposal of animal carcasses are the same whether Santeria
sacrifice or some nonreligious killing preceded it. The city

does not, however, prohibit hunters from bringing their kill to their houses, nor does it regulate disposal after their activity. Despite substantial testimony at trial that the same public health hazards result from improper disposal of garbage by restaurants, restaurants are outside the scope of the ordinances. Improper disposal is a general problem that causes substantial health risks, but which respondent addresses only when it results from religious exercise. . . .

We conclude, in sum, that each of Hialeah's ordinances pursues the city's governmental interests only against conduct motivated by religious belief. . . . This precise evil is what the requirement of general applicability is designed to prevent.

III

A law burdening religious practice that is not neutral or not of general application must undergo the most rigorous of scrutiny. To satisfy the commands of the First Amendment, a law restrictive of religious practice must advance "'interests of the highest order'" and must be narrowly tailored in pursuit of those interests. . . . A law that targets religious conduct for distinctive treatment or advances legitimate governmental interests only against conduct with a religious motivation will survive strict scrutiny only in rare cases. It follows from what we have already said that these ordinances cannot withstand this scrutiny.

First, even were the governmental interests compelling, the ordinances are not drawn in narrow terms to accomplish those interests. . . .

Respondent has not demonstrated, moreover, that, in the context of these ordinances, its governmental interests are

compelling. Where government restricts only conduct protected by the First Amendment and fails to enact feasible
measures to restrict other conduct producing substantial
harm or alleged harm of the same sort, the interest given in
justification of the restriction is not compelling. . . .

IV

The Free Exercise Clause commits government itself to religious tolerance, and upon even slight suspicion that proposals for state intervention stem from animosity to religion or
distrust of its practices, all officials must pause to remember
their own high duty to the Constitution and to the rights it
secures. Those in office must be resolute in resisting impor-
tunate demands and must ensure that the sole reasons for
imposing the burdens of law and regulation are secular. Legislators may not devise mechanisms, overt or disguised, designed to persecute or oppress a religion or its practices. The
laws here in question were enacted contrary to these constitutional principles, and they are void.

Reversed.

Burwell v. Hobby
Lobby Stores (2014)

In 1993, Congress, in response to what it thought was the Court's insufficient protection of religious freedom, passed the Religious Freedom Restoration Act. The act created some exemptions from laws passed by Congress, even though the Court had stopped protecting those entitlements to exemptions as a matter of constitutional law. The devout owners of the Hobby Lobby corporation argued that their religious beliefs were adversely affected by the Affordable Care Act's requirement that businesses of their size provide birth control coverage to their employees, and that under RFRA, they should be exempt from the mandate. Hobby Lobby won the case and was granted the exemption.

Justice Alito delivered the opinion of the Court.

We must decide in these cases whether the Religious Freedom Restoration Act of 1993 (RFRA), permits the United States Department of Health and Human Services (HHS) to demand that three closely held corporations provide health-insurance coverage for methods of contraception that violate the sincerely held religious beliefs of the companies' owners.

We hold that the regulations that impose this obligation violate RFRA, which prohibits the Federal Government from taking any action that substantially burdens the exercise of religion unless that action constitutes the least restrictive means of serving a compelling government interest. . . .

I

A

Congress enacted RFRA in 1993 in order to provide very broad protection for religious liberty. . . .

. . . In order to ensure broad protection for religious liberty, RFRA provides that "Government shall not substantially burden a person's exercise of religion even if the burden results from a rule of general applicability." If the Government substantially burdens a person's exercise of religion, under the Act that person is entitled to an exemption from the rule unless the Government "demonstrates that application of the burden to the person—(1) is in furtherance of a compelling governmental interest; and (2) is the least restrictive means of furthering that compelling governmental interest." . . .

B

At issue in these cases are HHS regulations promulgated under the Patient Protection and Affordable Care Act of 2010 (ACA). . . .

Unless an exception applies, ACA requires an employer's group health plan or group-health-insurance coverage to furnish "preventive care and screenings" for women without "any cost sharing requirements." . . . Congress authorized the

Health Resources and Services Administration (HRSA), a component of HHS, to make that important and sensitive decision. . . .

In August 2011, . . . the HRSA promulgated the Women's Preventive Services Guidelines. The Guidelines provide that nonexempt employers are generally required to provide "coverage, without cost sharing" for "[a]ll Food and Drug Administration [(FDA)] approved contraceptive methods, sterilization procedures, and patient education and counseling." Although many of the required, FDA-approved methods of contraception work by preventing the fertilization of an egg, four of those methods (those specifically at issue in these cases) may have the effect of preventing an already fertilized egg from developing any further by inhibiting its attachment to the uterus.

HHS also authorized the HRSA to establish exemptions from the contraceptive mandate for "religious employers." That category encompasses "churches, their integrated auxiliaries, and conventions or associations of churches," as well as "the exclusively religious activities of any religious order."

In addition, HHS has effectively exempted certain religious nonprofit organizations, described under HHS regulations as "eligible organizations," from the contraceptive mandate. . . .

In addition to these exemptions for religious organizations, ACA exempts a great many employers from most of its coverage requirements. Employers providing "grandfathered health plans"—those that existed prior to March 23, 2010, and that have not made specified changes after that date—need not comply with many of the Act's requirements, including the contraceptive mandate. And employers with fewer than 50 employees are not required to provide health insurance at all. . . .

II

A

Norman and Elizabeth Hahn and their three sons are devout members of the Mennonite Church, a Christian denomination. The Mennonite Church opposes abortion and believes that "[t]he fetus in its earliest stages . . . shares humanity with those who conceived it."

Fifty years ago, Norman Hahn started a wood-working business in his garage, and since then, this company, Conestoga Wood Specialties, has grown and now has 950 employees. Conestoga is organized under Pennsylvania law as a for-profit corporation. The Hahns exercise sole ownership of the closely held business; they control its board of directors and hold all of its voting shares. One of the Hahn sons serves as the president and CEO.

The Hahns believe that they are required to run their business "in accordance with their religious beliefs and moral principles." To that end, the company's mission, as they see it, is to "operate in a professional environment founded upon the highest ethical, moral, and Christian principles." The company's "Vision and Values Statements" affirms that Conestoga endeavors to "ensur[e] a reasonable profit in [a] manner that reflects [the Hahns'] Christian heritage."

As explained in Conestoga's board-adopted "Statement on the Sanctity of Human Life," the Hahns believe that "human life begins at conception." It is therefore "against [their] moral conviction to be involved in the termination of human life" after conception, which they believe is a "sin against God to which they are held accountable." The Hahns have accordingly excluded from the group-health-insurance plan they offer to their employees certain contraceptive methods that they consider to be abortifacients.

The Hahns and Conestoga sued HHS and other federal officials and agencies under RFRA and the Free Exercise Clause of the First Amendment, seeking to enjoin application of ACA's contraceptive mandate insofar as it requires them to provide health-insurance coverage for four FDA-approved contraceptives that may operate after the fertilization of an egg. These include two forms of emergency contraception commonly called "morning after" pills and two types of intrauterine devices.

In opposing the requirement to provide coverage for the contraceptives to which they object, the Hahns argued that "it is immoral and sinful for [them] to intentionally participate in, pay for, facilitate, or otherwise support these drugs." . . .

B

David and Barbara Green and their three children are Christians who own and operate two family businesses. Forty-five years ago, David Green started an arts-and-crafts store that has grown into a nationwide chain called Hobby Lobby. There are now 500 Hobby Lobby stores, and the company has more than 13,000 employees. Hobby Lobby is organized as a for-profit corporation under Oklahoma law.

One of David's sons started an affiliated business, Mardel, which operates 35 Christian bookstores and employs close to 400 people. Mardel is also organized as a for-profit corporation under Oklahoma law. . . .

Hobby Lobby's statement of purpose commits the Greens to "[h]onoring the Lord in all [they] do by operating the company in a manner consistent with Biblical principles." . . .

Like the Hahns, the Greens believe that life begins at conception and that it would violate their religion to facilitate access to contraceptive drugs or devices that operate after that point. They specifically object to the same four contraceptive methods as the Hahns and, like the Hahns, they have no objection to the other 16 FDA-approved methods of birth control. . . .

The Greens, Hobby Lobby, and Mardel sued HHS and other federal agencies and officials to challenge the contraceptive mandate under RFRA and the Free Exercise Clause. . . .

III

A

RFRA prohibits the "Government [from] substantially burden[ing] a person's exercise of religion even if the burden results from a rule of general applicability" unless the Government "demonstrates that application of the burden to the person—(1) is in furtherance of a compelling governmental interest; and (2) is the least restrictive means of furthering that compelling governmental interest." The first question that we must address is whether this provision applies to regulations that govern the activities of for-profit corporations like Hobby Lobby, Conestoga, and Mardel.

HHS contends that neither these companies nor their owners can even be heard under RFRA. According to HHS, the companies cannot sue because they seek to make a profit for their owners, and the owners cannot be heard because the regulations, at least as a formal matter, apply only to the companies and not to the owners as individuals. HHS's argument would have dramatic consequences. . . .

. . . Congress provided protection for people like the Hahns and Greens by employing a familiar legal fiction: It included corporations within RFRA's definition of "persons." But it is important to keep in mind that the purpose of this fiction is to provide protection for human beings. A corporation is simply a form of organization used by human beings to achieve desired ends. An established body of law specifies the rights and obligations of the people (including shareholders, officers, and employees) who are associated with a corporation in one way or another. When rights, whether constitutional or statutory, are extended to corporations, the purpose is to protect the rights of these people. . . . Protecting corporations from government seizure of their property without just compensation protects all those who have a stake in the corporations' financial well-being. And protecting the free-exercise rights of corporations like Hobby Lobby, Conestoga, and Mardel protects the religious liberty of the humans who own and control those companies. . . .

IV

Because RFRA applies in these cases, we must next ask whether the HHS contraceptive mandate "substantially burden[s]" the exercise of religion. We have little trouble concluding that it does.

A

As we have noted, the Hahns and Greens have a sincere religious belief that life begins at conception. They therefore object on religious grounds to providing health insurance that covers methods of birth control that, as HHS acknowledges, may result in the destruction of an embryo. By requiring the Hahns and Greens and their companies to arrange for such coverage, the HHS mandate demands that they engage in conduct that seriously violates their religious beliefs.

If the Hahns and Greens and their companies do not yield to this demand, the economic consequences will be severe. If the companies continue to offer group health plans that do not cover the contraceptives at issue, they will be taxed $100 per day for each affected individual. For Hobby Lobby, the bill could amount to $1.3 million per day or about $475 million per year; for Conestoga, the assessment could be $90,000 per day or $33 million per year; and for Mardel, it could be $40,000 per day or about $15 million per year. These sums are surely substantial.

It is true that the plaintiffs could avoid these assessments by dropping insurance coverage altogether and thus forcing their employees to obtain health insurance on one of the exchanges established under ACA. But if at least one of their full-time employees were to qualify for a subsidy on one of the government-run exchanges, this course would also entail substantial economic consequences. The companies could face penalties of $2,000 per employee each year. These penalties would amount to roughly $26 million for Hobby Lobby, $1.8 million for Conestoga, and $800,000 for Mardel. . . .

C

In taking the position that the HHS mandate does not impose a substantial burden on the exercise of religion, HHS's main argument (echoed by the principal dissent) is basically that the connection between what the objecting parties must do (provide health-insurance coverage for four methods of contraception that may operate after the fertilization of an egg) and the end that they find to be morally wrong (destruction of an embryo) is simply too attenuated. HHS and the dissent note that providing the coverage would not itself result in the destruction of an embryo; that would occur only if an employee chose to take advantage of the coverage and to use one of the four methods at issue.

This argument dodges the question that RFRA presents (whether the HHS mandate imposes a substantial burden on the ability of the objecting parties to conduct business in accordance with their religious beliefs) and instead addresses a very different question that the federal courts have no business addressing (whether the religious belief asserted in a RFRA case is reasonable). The Hahns and Greens believe that providing the coverage demanded by the HHS regulations is connected to the destruction of an embryo in a way that is sufficient to make it immoral for them to provide the coverage. This belief implicates a difficult and important question of religion and moral philosophy, namely, the circumstances under which it is wrong for a person to perform an act that is innocent in itself but that has the effect of enabling or facilitating the commission of an immoral act by another. Arrogating the authority to provide a binding national answer to this religious and philosophical question, HHS and the principal dissent in effect tell the plaintiffs that their beliefs are flawed. For good reason, we have repeatedly refused to take such a step. . . .

Similarly, in these cases, the Hahns and Greens and their companies sincerely believe that providing the insurance coverage demanded by the HHS regulations lies on the forbidden side of the line, and it is not for us to say that their religious beliefs are mistaken or insubstantial. Instead, our "narrow function . . . in this context is to determine" whether the line drawn reflects "an honest conviction," and there is no dispute that it does. . . .

V

Since the HHS contraceptive mandate imposes a substantial burden on the exercise of religion, we must move on and decide whether HHS has shown that the mandate both "(1) is in furtherance of a compelling governmental interest; and (2) is the least restrictive means of furthering that compelling governmental interest."

A

HHS asserts that the contraceptive mandate serves a variety of important interests, but many of these are couched in very broad terms, such as promoting "public health" and "gender equality." . . .

. . . HHS maintains that the mandate serves a compelling interest in ensuring that all women have access to all FDA-approved contraceptives without cost sharing. . . .

. . . We will assume that the interest in guaranteeing cost-free access to the four challenged contraceptive methods is compelling within the meaning of RFRA, and we will proceed to consider the final prong of the RFRA test, i.e., whether HHS has shown that the contraceptive mandate is "the least restrictive means of furthering that compelling governmental interest."

B

The least-restrictive-means standard is exceptionally demanding, and it is not satisfied here. HHS has not shown that it lacks other means of achieving its desired goal without imposing a substantial burden on the exercise of religion by the objecting parties in these cases.

The most straightforward way of doing this would be for the Government to assume the cost of providing the four contraceptives at issue to any women who are unable to obtain them under their health-insurance policies due to their employers' religious objections. This would certainly be less restrictive of the plaintiffs' religious liberty, and HHS has not shown that this is not a viable alternative. HHS has not provided any estimate of the average cost per employee of providing access to these contraceptives, two of which, according to the FDA, are designed primarily for emergency use. Nor has HHS provided any statistics regarding the number of employees who might be affected because they work for corporations like Hobby Lobby, Conestoga, and Mardel. Nor has HHS told us that it is unable to provide such statistics. It seems likely, however, that the cost of providing the forms of contraceptives at issue in these cases (if not all FDA-approved contraceptives) would be minor when compared with the overall cost of ACA. . . . [If,] as HHS tells us, providing all women with cost-free access to all FDA-approved methods of contraception is a Government interest of the highest order, it is hard to understand HHS's argument that it cannot be required under RFRA to pay anything in order to achieve this important goal. . . .

. . . [W]e need not rely on the option of a new, government-funded program in order to conclude that the HHS regulations fail the least-restrictive-means test. HHS itself has demonstrated that it has at its disposal an approach that is less restrictive than requiring employers to fund contraceptive methods that violate their religious beliefs. As we explained above, HHS has already established an accommodation for nonprofit organizations with religious objections. Under that accommodation, the organization can self-certify that it opposes providing coverage for particular contraceptive services. If the organization makes such a certification, the organization's insurance issuer or third-party administrator must "[e]xpressly exclude contraceptive coverage from the group health insurance coverage provided in connection with the group health plan" and "[p]rovide separate payments for any contraceptive services required to be covered" without imposing "any cost-sharing requirements . . . on the eligible organization, the group health plan, or plan participants or beneficiaries."

We do not decide today whether an approach of this type complies with RFRA for purposes of all religious claims. At a minimum, however, it does not impinge on the plaintiffs' religious belief that providing insurance coverage for the contraceptives at issue here violates their religion, and it serves HHS's stated interests equally well. . . .

C

HHS and the principal dissent argue that a ruling in favor of the objecting parties in these cases will lead to a flood of religious objections regarding a wide variety of medical procedures and drugs, such as vaccinations and blood transfusions, but HHS has made no effort to substantiate this prediction. HHS points to no evidence that insurance plans in existence prior to the enactment of ACA excluded coverage for such items. Nor has HHS provided evidence that any significant number of employers sought exemption, on religious grounds, from any of ACA's coverage requirements other than the contraceptive mandate.

It is HHS's apparent belief that no insurance-coverage mandate would violate RFRA—no matter how significantly it impinges on the religious liberties of employers—that would lead to intolerable consequences. Under HHS's view, RFRA would permit the Government to require all employers to provide coverage for any medical procedure allowed by law in the jurisdiction in question—for instance, third-trimester abortions or assisted suicide. The owners of many closely held corporations could not in good conscience provide such coverage, and thus HHS would effectively exclude these people from full participation in the economic life of the Nation. RFRA was enacted to prevent such an outcome.

In any event, our decision in these cases is concerned solely with the contraceptive mandate. Our decision should not be understood to hold that an insurance-coverage mandate must necessarily fall if it conflicts with an employer's religious beliefs. Other coverage requirements, such as immunizations, may be supported by different interests (for example, the need to combat the spread of infectious diseases) and may involve different arguments about the least restrictive means of providing them. . . .

——

The contraceptive mandate, as applied to closely held corporations, violates RFRA. Our decision on that statutory question makes it unnecessary to reach the First Amendment claim raised by Conestoga and the Hahns.

The judgment of the Tenth Circuit in No. 13–354 is affirmed; the judgment of the Third Circuit in No. 13–356 is reversed, and that case is remanded for further proceedings consistent with this opinion.

It is so ordered.

Holt v. Hobbs (2015)

> *In this case, the Court used a separate law, the Religious Land Use and Institutionalized Persons Act, to argue that Arkansas prison administrators had illegally limited the religious rights of a prisoner by attempting to force him to trim his beard under prison policy, despite the religious reasons he had for growing it. As in* Hobby Lobby, *here it was congressional legislation more than the Constitution itself that protected the rights of religious believers.*

Justice Alito delivered the opinion of the Court.

Petitioner Gregory Holt, also known as Abdul Maalik Muhammad, is an Arkansas inmate and a devout Muslim who wishes to grow a ½-inch beard in accordance with his religious beliefs. Petitioner's objection to shaving his beard clashes with the Arkansas Department of Correction's grooming policy, which prohibits inmates from growing beards unless they have a particular dermatological condition. We hold that the Department's policy, as applied in this case, violates the Religious Land Use and Institutionalized Persons Act of 2000 (RLUIPA), which prohibits a state or local government from taking any action that substantially burdens the religious exercise of an institutionalized person unless the government demonstrates that the action constitutes the least restrictive means of furthering a compelling governmental interest.

We conclude in this case that the Department's policy substantially burdens petitioner's religious exercise. Although we do not question the importance of the Department's interests in stopping the flow of contraband and facilitating prisoner identification, we do doubt whether the prohibition against petitioner's beard furthers its compelling interest about contraband. And we conclude that the Department has failed to show that its policy is the least restrictive means of furthering its compelling interests. We thus reverse the decision of the United States Court of Appeals for the Eighth Circuit.

I

A

Congress enacted RLUIPA and its sister statute, the Religious Freedom Restoration Act of 1993 (RFRA), "in order to provide very broad protection for religious liberty." . . .

. . . Congress enacted RFRA in order to provide greater protection for religious exercise than is available under the First Amendment. . . . In making RFRA applicable to the States and their subdivisions, Congress relied on Section 5 of the Fourteenth Amendment, but in *City of Boerne v. Flores* (1997), this Court held that RFRA exceeded Congress' powers under that provision.

Congress responded to *City of Boerne* by enacting RLUIPA, which applies to the States and their subdivisions and invokes congressional authority under the Spending and Commerce

Clauses. RLUIPA concerns two areas of government activity: Section 2 governs land-use regulation; and Section 3—the provision at issue in this case—governs religious exercise by institutionalized persons. . . . RLUIPA . . . allows prisoners "to seek religious accommodations pursuant to the same standard as set forth in RFRA."

Several provisions of RLUIPA underscore its expansive protection for religious liberty. Congress defined "religious exercise" capaciously to include "any exercise of religion, whether or not compelled by, or central to, a system of religious belief." Congress mandated that this concept "shall be construed in favor of a broad protection of religious exercise, to the maximum extent permitted by the terms of this chapter and the Constitution." And Congress stated that RLUIPA "may require a government to incur expenses in its own operations to avoid imposing a substantial burden on religious exercise."

B

Petitioner, as noted, is in the custody of the Arkansas Department of Correction and he objects on religious grounds to the Department's grooming policy, which provides that "[n]o inmates will be permitted to wear facial hair other than a neatly trimmed mustache that does not extend beyond the corner of the mouth or over the lip." The policy makes no exception for inmates who object on religious grounds, but it does contain an exemption for prisoners with medical needs. . . . The policy provides that "[f]ailure to abide by [the Department's] grooming standards is grounds for disciplinary action."

Petitioner sought permission to grow a beard and, although he believes that his faith requires him not to trim his beard at all, he proposed a "compromise" under which he would grow only a ½-inch beard. Prison officials denied his request, and the warden told him: "[Y]ou will abide by [Arkansas Department of Correction] policies and if you choose to disobey, you can suffer the consequences."

Petitioner filed a *pro se* complaint in Federal District Court challenging the grooming policy under RLUIPA. We refer to the respondent prison officials collectively as the Department. In October 2011, the District Court granted petitioner a preliminary injunction and remanded to a Magistrate Judge for an evidentiary hearing. At the hearing, the Department called two witnesses. Both expressed the belief that inmates could hide contraband in even a ½-inch beard, but neither pointed to any instances in which this had been done in Arkansas or elsewhere. . . .

II

Under RLUIPA, petitioner bore the initial burden of proving that the Department's grooming policy implicates his religious exercise. RLUIPA protects "any exercise of religion, whether or not compelled by, or central to, a system of religious belief," but, of course, a prisoner's request for an accommodation must be sincerely based on a religious belief and not some other motivation. Here, the religious exercise at issue is the growing of a beard, which petitioner believes is a dictate of his religious faith, and the Department does not dispute the sincerity of petitioner's belief.

In addition to showing that the relevant exercise of religion is grounded in a sincerely held religious belief, petitioner also bore the burden of proving that the Department's grooming policy substantially burdened that exercise of

religion. Petitioner easily satisfied that obligation. The Department's grooming policy requires petitioner to shave his
beard and thus to "engage in conduct that seriously violates
[his] religious beliefs." If petitioner contravenes that policy
and grows his beard, he will face serious disciplinary action.
Because the grooming policy puts petitioner to this choice, it
substantially burdens his religious exercise. Indeed, the Department does not argue otherwise. . . .

III

Since petitioner met his burden of showing that the Department's grooming policy substantially burdened his exercise of
religion, the burden shifted to the Department to show that
its refusal to allow petitioner to grow a ½-inch beard "(1) [was]
in furtherance of a compelling governmental interest; and
(2) [was] the least restrictive means of furthering that compelling governmental interest." . . .

The Department contends that enforcing this prohibition
is the least restrictive means of furthering prison safety and
security in two specific ways.

A

The Department first claims that the no-beard policy prevents prisoners from hiding contraband. The Department
worries that prisoners may use their beards to conceal all
manner of prohibited items, including razors, needles, drugs,
and cellular phone subscriber identity module (SIM) cards.

We readily agree that the Department has a compelling
interest in staunching the flow of contraband into and within
its facilities, but the argument that this interest would be

seriously compromised by allowing an inmate to grow a ½-inch beard is hard to take seriously. . . . An item of contraband would have to be very small indeed to be concealed by a ½-inch beard, and a prisoner seeking to hide an item in such a short beard would have to find a way to prevent the item from falling out. Since the Department does not demand that inmates have shaved heads or short crew cuts, it is hard to see why an inmate would seek to hide contraband in a ½-inch beard rather than in the longer hair on his head. . . .

The Department failed to establish that it could not satisfy its security concerns by simply searching petitioner's beard. The Department already searches prisoners' hair and clothing, and it presumably examines the ¼-inch beards of inmates with dermatological conditions. It has offered no sound reason why hair, clothing, and ¼-inch beards can be searched but ½-inch beards cannot. The Department suggests that requiring guards to search a prisoner's beard would pose a risk to the physical safety of a guard if a razor or needle was concealed in the beard. But that is no less true for searches of hair, clothing, and ¼-inch beards. And the Department has failed to prove that it could not adopt the less restrictive alternative of having the prisoner run a comb through his beard. For all these reasons, the Department's interest in eliminating contraband cannot sustain its refusal to allow petitioner to grow a ½-inch beard.

B

The Department contends that its grooming policy is necessary to further an additional compelling interest, i.e., preventing prisoners from disguising their identities. The Department tells us that the no-beard policy allows security officers to identify prisoners quickly and accurately. It claims that bearded inmates could shave their beards and change their appearance in order to enter restricted areas within the prison, to escape, and to evade apprehension after escaping. . . .

. . . [E]ven if we assume for present purposes that the Department's grooming policy sufficiently furthers its interest in the identification of prisoners, that policy still violates RLUIPA as applied in the circumstances present here. The Department contends that a prisoner who has a beard when he is photographed for identification purposes might confuse guards by shaving his beard. But as petitioner has argued, the Department could largely solve this problem by requiring that all inmates be photographed without beards when first admitted to the facility and, if necessary, periodically thereafter. Once that is done, an inmate like petitioner could be allowed to grow a short beard and could be photographed again when the beard reached the ½-inch limit. Prison guards would then have a bearded and clean-shaven photo to use in making identifications. In fact, the Department (like many other States) already has a policy of photographing a prisoner both when he enters an institution and when his "appearance changes at any time during [his] incarceration."

The Department argues that the dual-photo method is inadequate because, even if it might help authorities apprehend a bearded prisoner who escapes and then shaves his beard once outside the prison, this method is unlikely to assist guards when an inmate quickly shaves his beard in order to alter his appearance within the prison. The Department contends that the identification concern is particularly acute at petitioner's prison, where inmates live in barracks and work in fields. Counsel for the Department suggested at oral argument that a prisoner could gain entry to a restricted area by shaving his beard and swapping identification cards with another inmate while out in the fields.

We are unpersuaded by these arguments for at least two reasons. First, the Department failed to show, in the face of petitioner's evidence, that its prison system is so different from the many institutions that allow facial hair that the dual-photo method cannot be employed at its institutions. Second, the Department failed to establish why the risk that a prisoner will shave a ½-inch beard to disguise himself is so great that ½-inch beards cannot be allowed, even though prisoners are allowed to grow mustaches, head hair, or ¼-inch beards for medical reasons. All of these could also be shaved off at a moment's notice, but the Department apparently does not think that this possibility raises a serious security concern.

C

In addition to its failure to prove that petitioner's proposed alternatives would not sufficiently serve its security interests, the Department has not provided an adequate response to two additional arguments that implicate the RLUIPA analysis.

First, the Department has not adequately demonstrated why its grooming policy is substantially underinclusive in at least two respects. Although the Department denied petitioner's request to grow a ½-inch beard, it permits prisoners with a dermatological condition to grow ¼-inch beards. The Department does this even though both beards pose similar risks. And the Department permits inmates to grow more than a ½-inch of hair on their heads. With respect to hair length, the grooming policy provides only that hair must be worn "above the ear" and "no longer in the back than the middle of the nape of the neck." Hair on the head is a more plausible place to hide contraband than a ½-inch beard—and the same is true of an inmate's clothing and shoes. Nevertheless, the Department does not require inmates to go about bald, barefoot, or naked. . . .

In an attempt to demonstrate why its grooming policy is underinclusive in these respects, the Department emphasizes that petitioner's ½-inch beard is longer than the ¼-inch beard allowed for medical reasons. But the Department has failed to establish (and the District Court did not find) that a ¼-inch difference in beard length poses a meaningful increase in security risk. The Department also asserts that few inmates require beards for medical reasons while many may request beards for religious reasons. But the Department has not argued that denying petitioner an exemption is necessary to further a compelling interest in cost control or program administration. At bottom, this argument is but another formulation of the "classic rejoinder of bureaucrats throughout history: If I make an exception for you, I'll have to make one for everybody, so no exceptions." We have rejected a similar argument in analogous contexts, and we reject it again today.

Second, the Department failed to show, in the face of petitioner's evidence, why the vast majority of States and the Federal Government permit inmates to grow ½-inch beards, either for any reason or for religious reasons, but it cannot. . . . That so many other prisons allow inmates to grow beards while ensuring prison safety and security suggests that the Department could satisfy its security concerns through a means less restrictive than denying petitioner the exemption he seeks.

We do not suggest that RLUIPA requires a prison to grant a particular religious exemption as soon as a few other jurisdictions do so. But when so many prisons offer an accommodation, a prison must, at a minimum, offer persuasive reasons why it believes that it must take a different course, and the Department failed to make that showing here. . . .

We emphasize that although RLUIPA provides substantial protection for the religious exercise of institutionalized persons, it also affords prison officials ample ability to maintain security. We highlight three ways in which this is so. First, in applying RLUIPA's statutory standard, courts should not blind themselves to the fact that the analysis is conducted in the prison setting. Second, if an institution suspects that an inmate is using religious activity to cloak illicit conduct, "prison officials may appropriately question whether a prisoner's religiosity, asserted as the basis for a requested accommodation, is authentic." Third, even if a claimant's religious belief is sincere, an institution might be entitled to withdraw an accommodation if the claimant abuses the exemption in a manner that undermines the prison's compelling interests.

IV

In sum, we hold that the Department's grooming policy violates RLUIPA insofar as it prevents petitioner from growing a ½-inch beard in accordance with his religious beliefs. The judgment of the United States Court of Appeals for the Eighth Circuit is reversed, and the case is remanded for further proceedings consistent with this opinion.

It is so ordered.

Part IV

RELIGIOUS FREEDOM
and
DISCRIMINATION

"Islam Is Peace," by *President George W. Bush* (2001)

After the terrorist attacks in New York City and Washington, D.C., on September 11, 2001, pressure mounted on the sitting president, George W. Bush, to speak out not just against terrorism, but also against Islam, which some commentators were eager to blame for the heinous attacks. Bush flatly refused to do so. Instead, he delivered an address at the Islamic Center of Washington, D.C., defending Islam as a religion of peace and promoting the importance of religious freedom in America.

THE PRESIDENT: Thank you all very much for your hospitality. We've just had a—wide-ranging discussions on the matter at hand. Like the good folks standing with me, the American people were appalled and outraged at last Tuesday's attacks. And so were Muslims all across the world. Both Americans and Muslim friends and citizens, tax-paying citizens, and Muslims in other nations were just appalled and could not believe what we saw on our TV screens.

These acts of violence against innocents violate the fundamental tenets of the Islamic faith. And it's important for my fellow Americans to understand that.

The English translation is not as eloquent as the original Arabic, but let me quote from the Koran, itself: In the long run, evil in the extreme will be the end of those who do evil. For that they rejected the signs of Allah and held them up to ridicule.

The face of terror is not the true faith of Islam. That's not what Islam is all about. Islam is peace. These terrorists don't represent peace. They represent evil and war.

When we think of Islam we think of a faith that brings comfort to a billion people around the world. Billions of people find comfort and solace and peace. And that's made brothers and sisters out of every race—out of every race.

America counts millions of Muslims amongst our citizens, and Muslims make an incredibly valuable contribution to our country. Muslims are doctors, lawyers, law professors, members of the military, entrepreneurs, shopkeepers, moms and dads. And they need to be treated with respect. In our anger and emotion, our fellow Americans must treat each other with respect.

Women who cover their heads in this country must feel comfortable going outside their homes. Moms who wear cover must be not intimidated in America. That's not the America I know. That's not the America I value.

I've been told that some fear to leave; some don't want to go shopping for their families; some don't want to go about their ordinary daily routines because, by wearing cover, they're afraid they'll be intimidated. That should not and that will not stand in America.

Those who feel like they can intimidate our fellow citizens to take out their anger don't represent the best of America, they represent the worst of humankind, and they should be ashamed of that kind of behavior.

This is a great country. It's a great country because we

share the same values of respect and dignity and human worth. And it is my honor to be meeting with leaders who feel just the same way I do. They're outraged, they're sad. They love America just as much as I do.

I want to thank you all for giving me a chance to come by. And may God bless us all.

"A More Perfect Union," by
President Barack Obama (2008)

When Senator Barack Obama of Illinois sought the Democratic Party's nomination in the 2008 presidential election, he became one of the first Black Americans to run for the country's highest office. Race inevitably affected his campaign, and on March 18, he gave a speech tackling the challenges this presented head-on and addressing allegations that the views of his church's pastor regarding race and terrorism were anti-American. As part of the speech, Obama explains the importance of faith to his worldview and his connection to the Black community, and expounds on the ideal that people of all religions and all backgrounds have an equal place in the United States.

. . . "We the people, in order to form a more perfect union."

Two hundred and twenty one years ago, in a hall that still stands across the street, a group of men gathered and, with these simple words, launched America's improbable experiment in democracy.

Farmers and scholars, statesmen and patriots who had

traveled across the ocean to escape tyranny and persecution finally made real their declaration of independence at a Philadelphia convention that lasted through the spring of 1787.

The document they produced was eventually signed but ultimately unfinished. It was stained by this nation's original sin of slavery, a question that divided the colonies and brought the convention to a stalemate until the founders chose to allow the slave trade to continue for at least 20 more years, and to leave any final resolution to future generations.

Of course, the answer to the slavery question was already embedded within our Constitution—a Constitution that had at its very core the ideal of equal citizenship under the law; a Constitution that promised its people liberty and justice, and a union that could be and should be perfected over time.

And yet words on a parchment would not be enough to deliver slaves from bondage, or provide men and women of every color and creed their full rights and obligations as citizens of the United States.

What would be needed were Americans in successive generations who were willing to do their part—through protests and struggle, on the streets and in the courts, through a civil war and civil disobedience, and always at great risk—to narrow that gap between the promise of our ideals and the reality of their time. . . .

I chose to run for president at this moment in history because I believe deeply that we cannot solve the challenges of our time unless we solve them together, unless we perfect our union by understanding that we may have different stories, but we hold common hopes; that we may not look the same and may not have come from the same place, but we all want to move in the same direction: toward a better future for our children and our grandchildren.

And this belief comes from my unyielding faith in the decency and generosity of the American people. But it also comes from my own story. I am the son of a black man from Kenya and a white woman from Kansas. I was raised with the help of a white grandfather who survived a Depression to serve in Patton's army during World War II and a white grandmother who worked on a bomber assembly line at Fort Leavenworth while he was overseas.

I've gone to some of the best schools in America and I've lived in one of the world's poorest nations. I am married to a black American who carries within her the blood of slaves and slave owners, an inheritance we pass on to our two precious daughters.

I have brothers, sisters, nieces, nephews, uncles and cousins of every race and every hue scattered across three continents. And for as long as I live, I will never forget that in no other country on earth is my story even possible.

It's a story that hasn't made me the most conventional of candidates. But it is a story that has seared into my genetic makeup the idea that this nation is more than the sum of its parts—that out of many, we are truly one.

Throughout the first year of this campaign, against all predictions to the contrary, we saw how hungry the American people were for this message of unity. Despite the temptation to view my candidacy through a purely racial lens, we won commanding victories in states with some of the whitest populations in the country. In South Carolina, where the Confederate flag still flies, we built a powerful coalition of African Americans and white Americans.

This is not to say that race has not been an issue in this campaign. At various stages in the campaign, some commentators have deemed me either "too black" or "not black enough." . . .

And yet, it's only been in the last couple of weeks that the discussion of race in this campaign has taken a particularly divisive turn.

On one end of the spectrum, we've heard the implication that my candidacy is somehow an exercise in affirmative action; that it's based solely on the desire of wild- and wide-eyed liberals to purchase racial reconciliation on the cheap.

On the other end, we've heard my former pastor, Jeremiah Wright, use incendiary language to express views that have the potential not only to widen the racial divide, but views that denigrate both the greatness and the goodness of our nation and that rightly offend white and black alike.

I have already condemned, in unequivocal terms, the statements of Reverend Wright that have caused such controversy, and in some cases, pain. . . .

. . . Reverend Wright's comments were not only wrong but divisive, divisive at a time when we need unity; racially charged at a time when we need to come together to solve a set of monumental problems—two wars, a terrorist threat, a falling economy, a chronic health care crisis and potentially devastating climate change, problems that are neither black or white or Latino or Asian, but rather problems that confront us all.

Given my background, my politics, and my professed values and ideals, there will no doubt be those for whom my statements of condemnation are not enough.

Why associate myself with Reverend Wright in the first place, they may ask? Why not join another church? . . .

But the truth is, that isn't all that I know of the man. The man I met more than twenty years ago is a man who helped introduce me to my Christian faith, a man who spoke to me about our obligations to love one another; to care for the sick and lift up the poor. . . .

In my first book, *Dreams From My Father*, I described the experience of my first service at Trinity, and it goes as follows: "People began to shout, to rise from their seats and clap and cry out, a forceful wind carrying the reverend's voice up into the rafters.

"And in that single note—hope—I heard something else; at the foot of that cross, inside the thousands of churches across the city, I imagined the stories of ordinary black people merging with the stories of David and Goliath, Moses and Pharaoh, the Christians in the lion's den, Ezekiel's field of dry bones."

"Those stories of survival and freedom and hope became our story, my story. The blood that spilled was our blood; the tears our tears; until this black church, on this bright day, seemed once more a vessel carrying the story of a people into future generations and into a larger world.

"Our trials and triumphs became at once unique and universal, black and more than black. In chronicling our journey, the stories and songs gave us a meaning to reclaim memories that we didn't need to feel shame about—memories that all people might study and cherish and with which we could start to rebuild."

That has been my experience at Trinity. Like other predominantly black churches across the country, Trinity embodies the black community in its entirety—the doctor and the welfare mom, the model student and the former gangbanger.

Like other black churches, Trinity's services are full of raucous laughter and sometimes bawdy humor. They are full of dancing and clapping and screaming and shouting that may seem jarring to the untrained ear.

The church contains in full the kindness and cruelty, the fierce intelligence and the shocking ignorance, the struggles and successes, the love and, yes, the bitterness and biases that make up the black experience in America.

And this helps explain, perhaps, my relationship with Reverend Wright. As imperfect as he may be, he has been like family to me. He strengthened my faith, officiated my wedding and baptized my children.

Not once in my conversations with him have I heard him talk about any ethnic group in derogatory terms or treat whites with whom he interacted with anything but courtesy and respect.

He contains within him the contradictions—the good and the bad—of the community that he has served diligently for so many years.

I can no more disown him than I can disown the black community. I can no more disown him than I can disown my white grandmother, a woman who helped raise me, a woman who sacrificed again and again for me, a woman who loves me as much as she loves anything in this world, but a woman who once confessed her fear of black men who passed her by on the street, and who on more than one occasion has uttered racial or ethnic stereotypes that made me cringe.

These people are a part of me. And they are part of America, this country that I love. . . .

. . . [T]he issues that have surfaced over the last few weeks reflect the complexities of race in this country that we've never really worked through, a part of our union that we have not yet made perfect.

And if we walk away now, if we simply retreat into our respective corners, we will never be able to come together and solve challenges like health care or education or the need to find good jobs for every American.

Understanding this reality requires a reminder of how we

arrived at this point. As William Faulkner once wrote, "The past isn't dead and buried. In fact, it isn't even past."

We do not need to recite here the history of racial injustice in this country.

But we do need to remind ourselves that so many of the disparities that exist between the African-American community and the larger American community today can be traced directly to inequalities passed on from an earlier generation that suffered under the brutal legacy of slavery and Jim Crow.

Segregated schools were, and are, inferior schools. We still haven't fixed them, 50 years after *Brown v. Board of Education*.

And the inferior education they provided, then and now, helps explain the pervasive achievement gap between today's black and white students.

Legalized discrimination, where blacks were prevented, often through violence, from owning property, or loans were not granted to African-American business owners, or black homeowners could not access FHA mortgages, or blacks were excluded from unions or the police force or the fire department, meant that black families could not amass any meaningful wealth to bequeath to future generations.

That history helps explain the wealth and income gap between blacks and whites and the concentrated pockets of poverty that persist in so many of today's urban and rural communities.

A lack of economic opportunity among black men and the shame and frustration that came from not being able to provide for one's family contributed to the erosion of black families, a problem that welfare policies for many years may have worsened.

And the lack of basic services in so many urban black

neighborhoods—parks for kids to play in, police walking the beat, regular garbage pickup, building code enforcement—all help create a cycle of violence, blight and neglect that continues to haunt us.

This is the reality in which Reverend Wright and other African-Americans of his generation grew up. They came of age in the late '50s and early '60s, a time when segregation was still the law of the land and opportunity was systematically constricted.

What's remarkable is not how many failed in the face of discrimination, but how many men and women overcame the odds; how many were able to make a way out of no way for those like me who would come after them.

But for all those who scratched and clawed their way to get a piece of the American Dream, there were many who didn't make it—those who were ultimately defeated, in one way or another, by discrimination. That legacy of defeat was passed on to future generations—those young men and increasingly young women who we see standing on street corners or languishing in our prisons, without hope or prospects for the future.

Even for those blacks who did make it, questions of race, and racism, continue to define their world view in fundamental ways. For the men and women of Reverend Wright's generation, the memories of humiliation and doubt and fear have not gone away; nor has the anger and the bitterness of those years. . . .

That anger is not always productive. Indeed, all too often it distracts attention from solving real problems. It keeps us from squarely facing our own complicity within the African-American community in our condition, it prevents the African-American community from forging the alliances it needs to bring about real change.

But the anger is real, it is powerful, and to simply wish it away, to condemn it without understanding its roots only serves to widen the chasm of misunderstanding that exists between the races.

In fact, a similar anger exists within segments of the white community. Most working- and middle-class white Americans don't feel that they have been particularly privileged by their race.

Their experience is the immigrant experience. As far as they're concerned, no one handed them anything, they built it from scratch. They've worked hard all their lives, many times only to see their jobs shipped overseas or their pensions dumped after a lifetime of labor. They are anxious about their futures, and they feel their dreams slipping away. And in an era of stagnant wages and global competition, opportunity comes to be seen as a zero-sum game, in which your dreams come at my expense.

So when they are told to bus their children to a school across town, when they hear that an African American is getting an advantage in landing a good job or a spot in a good college because of an injustice that they themselves never committed, when they're told that their fears about crime in urban neighborhoods are somehow prejudice, resentment builds over time.

Like the anger within the black community, these resentments aren't always expressed in polite company. But they have helped shape the political landscape for at least a generation. . . .

And just as black anger often proved counterproductive, so have these white resentments distracted attention from the real culprits of the middle-class squeeze: a corporate culture rife with inside dealing and questionable accounting practices and short-term greed; a Washington dominated by lobbyists and special interests; economic policies that favor the few over the many.

And yet, to wish away the resentments of white Americans, to label them as misguided or even racist without recognizing they are grounded in legitimate concerns, this, too, widens the racial divide and blocks the path to understanding.

This is where we are right now. It's a racial stalemate we've been stuck in for years. And contrary to the claims of some of my critics, black and white, I have never been so naive as to believe that we can get beyond our racial divisions in a single election cycle or with a single candidate, particularly . . . a candidacy as imperfect as my own.

But I have asserted a firm conviction, a conviction rooted in my faith in God and my faith in the American people, that, working together, we can move beyond some of our old racial wounds and that, in fact, we have no choice—we have no choice if we are to continue on the path of a more perfect union.

For the African-American community, that path means embracing the burdens of our past without becoming victims of our past. It means continuing to insist on a full measure of justice in every aspect of American life.

But it also means binding our particular grievances, for better health care and better schools and better jobs, to the larger aspirations of all Americans—the white woman struggling to break the glass ceiling, the white man who's been laid off, the immigrant trying to feed his family.

And it means also taking full responsibility for own lives—by demanding more from our fathers, and spending more time with our children, and reading to them, and teaching them that while they may face challenges and discrimination in their own lives, they must never succumb to despair or cynicism; they must always believe . . .

The profound mistake of Reverend Wright's sermons is not that he spoke about racism in our society. It's that he spoke as if our society was static; as if no progress had been made; as if this country—a country that has made it possible for one of his own members to run for the highest office in the land and build a coalition of white and black, Latino, and Asian, rich and poor, young and old—is still irrevocably bound to a tragic past.

What we know—what we have seen—is that America can change.

America can change. That is true genius of this nation. What we have already achieved gives us hope—the audacity to hope—for what we can and must achieve tomorrow.

Now, in the white community, the path to a more perfect union means acknowledging that what ails the African-American community does not just exist in the minds of black people; that the legacy of discrimination—and current incidents of discrimination, while less overt than in the past—that these things are real and must be addressed.

Not just with words, but with deeds—by investing in our schools and our communities; by enforcing our civil rights laws and ensuring fairness in our criminal justice system; by providing this generation with ladders of opportunity that were unavailable for previous generations.

It requires all Americans to realize that your dreams do not have to come at the expense of my dreams, that investing in the health, welfare, and education of black and brown and white children will ultimately help all of America prosper.

In the end, then, what is called for is nothing more and nothing less than what all the world's great religions demand: that we do unto others as we would have them do unto us.

Let us be our brother's keeper, Scripture tells us. Let us

be our sister's keeper. Let us find that common stake we all have in one another, and let our politics reflect that spirit as well.

For we have a choice in this country. We can accept a politics that breeds division and conflict and cynicism. We can tackle race only as spectacle, as we did in the OJ trial; or in the wake of tragedy, as we did in the aftermath of Katrina; or as fodder for the nightly news.

We can play Reverend Wright's sermons on every channel every day and talk about them from now until the election, and make the only question in this campaign whether or not the American people think that I somehow believe or sympathize with his most offensive words. . . .

We can do that. But if we do, I can tell you that in the next election, we'll be talking about some other distraction, and then another one, and then another one. And nothing will change.

That is one option.

Or, at this moment, in this election, we can come together and say, "Not this time."

This time we want to talk about the crumbling schools that are stealing the future of black children and white children and Asian children and Hispanic children and Native American children.

This time we want to reject the cynicism that tells us that these kids can't learn; that those kids who don't look like us are somebody else's problem.

The children of America are not those kids; they are our kids, and we will not let them fall behind in a 21st-century economy. Not this time.

This time we want to talk about how the lines in the emergency room are filled with whites and blacks and Hispanics who do not have health care, who don't have the power on their own to overcome the special interests in Washington, but who can take them on if we do it together.

This time we want to talk about the shuttered mills that once provided a decent life for men and women of every race, and the homes for sale that once belonged to Americans from every religion, every region, every walk of life.

This time we want to talk about the fact that the real problem is not that someone who doesn't look like you might take your job; it's that the corporation you work for will ship it overseas for nothing more than a profit. . . .

This time we want to talk about the men and women of every color and creed who serve together, and fight together, and bleed together under the same proud flag. We want to talk about how to bring them home from a war that should've never been authorized and should've never been waged.

And we want to talk about how we'll show our patriotism by caring for them, and their families, and giving them the benefits that they have earned.

I would not be running for president if I didn't believe with all my heart that this is what the vast majority of Americans want for this country. This union may never be perfect, but generation after generation has shown that it can always be perfected.

And today, whenever I find myself feeling doubtful or cynical about this possibility, what gives me the most hope is the next generation—the young people whose attitudes and beliefs and openness to change have already made history in this election. . . .

"Executive Order Protecting the Nation from Foreign Terrorist Entry into the United States," by *President Donald J. Trump* (2017)

A major twenty-first-century religious freedom controversy was sparked by President Trump's travel ban restricting the ability of people from several Muslim-majority countries to enter the United States. Opponents of the ban referenced the fact that Trump had made campaign statements suggesting he might prohibit Muslims from entering the United States and argued that its essential targeting of a religious group violated the Establishment and Free Exercise Clauses.

By the authority vested in me as President by the Constitution and laws of the United States of America, including the Immigration and Nationality Act (INA), and section 301 of title 3, United States Code, and to protect the American people from terrorist attacks by foreign nationals admitted to the United States, it is hereby ordered as follows:

Section 1. Purpose. The visa-issuance process plays a crucial role in detecting individuals with terrorist ties and stopping them from entering the United States. Perhaps in no instance was that more apparent than the terrorist attacks of

September 11, 2001, when State Department policy prevented consular officers from properly scrutinizing the visa applications of several of the 19 foreign nationals who went on to murder nearly 3,000 Americans. And while the visa-issuance process was reviewed and amended after the September 11 attacks to better detect would-be terrorists from receiving visas, these measures did not stop attacks by foreign nationals who were admitted to the United States.

Numerous foreign-born individuals have been convicted or implicated in terrorism-related crimes since September 11, 2001, including foreign nationals who entered the United States after receiving visitor, student, or employment visas, or who entered through the United States refugee resettlement program. Deteriorating conditions in certain countries due to war, strife, disaster, and civil unrest increase the likelihood that terrorists will use any means possible to enter the United States. The United States must be vigilant during the visa-issuance process to ensure that those approved for admission do not intend to harm Americans and that they have no ties to terrorism.

In order to protect Americans, the United States must ensure that those admitted to this country do not bear hostile attitudes toward it and its founding principles. The United States cannot, and should not, admit those who do not support the Constitution, or those who would place violent ideologies over American law. In addition, the United States should not admit those who engage in acts of bigotry or hatred (including "honor" killings, other forms of violence against women, or the persecution of those who practice religions different from their own) or those who would oppress Americans of any race, gender, or sexual orientation. . . .

Sec. 3. Suspension of Issuance of Visas and Other Immigration Benefits to Nationals of Countries of Particular

Concern. (a) The Secretary of Homeland Security, in consultation with the Secretary of State and the Director of National Intelligence, shall immediately conduct a review to determine the information needed from any country to adjudicate any visa, admission, or other benefit under the INA (adjudications) in order to determine that the individual seeking the benefit is who the individual claims to be and is not a security or public-safety threat.

(b) The Secretary of Homeland Security, in consultation with the Secretary of State and the Director of National Intelligence, shall submit to the President a report on the results of the review described in subsection (a) of this section, including the Secretary of Homeland Security's determination of the information needed for adjudications and a list of countries that do not provide adequate information, within 30 days of the date of this order. The Secretary of Homeland Security shall provide a copy of the report to the Secretary of State and the Director of National Intelligence.

(c) To temporarily reduce investigative burdens on relevant agencies during the review period described in subsection (a) of this section, to ensure the proper review and maximum utilization of available resources for the screening of foreign nationals, and to ensure that adequate standards are established to prevent infiltration by foreign terrorists or criminals, pursuant to section 212(f) of the INA, I hereby proclaim that the immigrant and nonimmigrant entry into the United States of aliens from countries referred to in section 217(a)(12) of the INA would be detrimental to the interests of the United States, and I hereby suspend entry into the United States, as immigrants and nonimmigrants, of such persons for 90 days from the date of this order (excluding those foreign nationals traveling on diplomatic visas, North Atlantic Treaty Organization visas, C-2 visas for travel to the United Nations, and G-1, G-2, G-3, and G-4 visas). . . .

Sec. 4. Implementing Uniform Screening Standards for All Immigration Programs. (a) The Secretary of State, the Secretary of Homeland Security, the Director of National Intelligence, and the Director of the Federal Bureau of Investigation shall implement a program, as part of the adjudication process for immigration benefits, to identify individuals seeking to enter the United States on a fraudulent basis with the intent to cause harm, or who are at risk of causing harm subsequent to their admission. This program will include the development of a uniform screening standard and procedure, such as in-person interviews; a database of identity documents proffered by applicants to ensure that duplicate documents are not used by multiple applicants; amended application forms that include questions aimed at identifying fraudulent answers and malicious intent; a mechanism to ensure that the applicant is who the applicant claims to be; a process to evaluate the applicant's likelihood of becoming a positively contributing member of society and the applicant's ability to make contributions to the national interest; and a mechanism to assess whether or not the applicant has the intent to commit criminal or terrorist acts after entering the United States. . . .

Sec. 5. Realignment of the U.S. Refugee Admissions Program for Fiscal Year 2017. (a) The Secretary of State shall suspend the U.S. Refugee Admissions Program (USRAP) for 120 days. During the 120-day period, the Secretary of State, in conjunction with the Secretary of Homeland Security and in consultation with the Director of National Intelligence, shall review the USRAP application and adjudication process to determine what additional procedures should be taken to ensure that those approved for refugee admission do not pose a threat to the security and welfare of the United States, and shall implement such additional procedures. Refugee applicants who are already in the USRAP process may be admitted upon the initiation and completion of these revised procedures. Upon the date that is 120 days after the date of this order, the Secretary of State shall resume USRAP admissions only for nationals of countries for which the Secretary of State, the Secretary of Homeland Security, and the Director of National Intelligence have jointly determined that such additional procedures are adequate to ensure the security and welfare of the United States. . . .

(c) Pursuant to section 212(f) of the INA, I hereby proclaim that the entry of nationals of Syria as refugees is detrimental to the interests of the United States and thus suspend any such entry until such time as I have determined that sufficient changes have been made to the USRAP to ensure that admission of Syrian refugees is consistent with the national interest.

(d) Pursuant to section 212(f) of the INA, I hereby proclaim that the entry of more than 50,000 refugees in fiscal year 2017 would be detrimental to the interests of the United States, and thus suspend any such entry until such time as I determine that additional admissions would be in the national interest. . . .

Sec. 10. Transparency and Data Collection. (a) To be more transparent with the American people, and to more effectively implement policies and practices that serve the national interest, the Secretary of Homeland Security, in consultation with the Attorney General, shall, consistent with applicable law and national security, collect and make publicly available within 180 days, and every 180 days thereafter:

(i) information regarding the number of foreign nationals

in the United States who have been charged with terrorism-related offenses while in the United States; convicted of terrorism-related offenses while in the United States; or removed from the United States based on terrorism-related activity, affiliation, or material support to a terrorism-related organization, or any other national security reasons since the date of this order or the last reporting period, whichever is later;

(ii) information regarding the number of foreign nationals in the United States who have been radicalized after entry into the United States and engaged in terrorism-related acts, or who have provided material support to terrorism-related organizations in countries that pose a threat to the United States, since the date of this order or the last reporting period, whichever is later; and

(iii) information regarding the number and types of acts of gender-based violence against women, including honor killings, in the United States by foreign nationals, since the date of this order or the last reporting period, whichever is later; and

(iv) any other information relevant to public safety and security as determined by the Secretary of Homeland Security and the Attorney General, including information on the immigration status of foreign nationals charged with major offenses.

Brief of Constitutional Law Scholars as Amicus Curiae in *Trump v. Hawaii* (2018)

President Trump's travel ban, excerpted above, met immediate legal resistance. The following is an amicus curiae—or "friend of the court"—brief written by attorney Joshua Matz and legal scholars Nelson Tebbe, Micah Schwartzman, and Corey Brettschneider (myself), and cosigned by more than forty-five scholars of religious freedom. We argued that the travel ban amounted to a form of institutionalized religious animus that was incompatible with the Constitution's ideals of the freedom of religion.

SUMMARY OF ARGUMENT

The Fourth Circuit properly protected religious liberty by affirming a preliminary injunction against Executive Order No. 13,780. Relying on *McCreary County v. ACLU of Ky.* (2005), and *Lemon v. Kurtzman* (1971), it held that the Order is unconstitutional because a "reasonable observer would likely conclude that [its] primary purpose is to exclude persons from the United States on the basis of their religious beliefs." *Under settled law, that ruling should be affirmed.*

But the Fourth Circuit also concluded that the Order cannot stand under a distinct legal principle—repeatedly confirmed in Religion Clause cases—that forbids the government from acting on the basis of animus toward any particular religious group. This fundamental rule has been recognized by jurists of many different persuasions in Establishment Clause cases. And as the Fourth Circuit concluded, it is directly applicable here.

Indeed, while the Fourth Circuit focused on *Lemon*'s secular purpose requirement, the facts that it considered even more clearly demonstrate anti-Muslim animus under familiar means of discerning improper motive. That conclusion is compelling based solely on President Trump's *post*-inauguration statements. But it is even more forcefully confirmed by a careful review of his *pre*-inauguration admissions of anti-Muslim animus—which, under precedent, must be considered as part of the legal analysis, and which are necessarily incorporated by reference into more recent presidential statements.

The extraordinary record in this case demonstrates that President Trump's principal motive in issuing the Order—and in gerrymandering it in peculiar ways—was anti-Muslim animus. After repeatedly promising voters during the campaign that he would ban Muslims from entering the United States, upon taking office, President Trump promptly issued a sweeping, unprecedented, and bizarrely-structured order with no discernible connection to an actual national security threat. While not *explicitly* denominated a "Muslim Ban," the Order (even as subsequently revised) came close enough to realizing that goal to satisfy his anti-Muslim election-season promise. And in case the point somehow remained unclear, President Trump has since made numerous statements—as recently as a series of tweets on June 5, 2017—to the effect that excluding Muslims was the Order's true purpose. An extensive public record thus establishes that in issuing the Order, President Trump was following through on his animus-laden campaign promise, rather than acting for any constitutionally legitimate reason.

While the Government appears keen to distance itself from the President's troubling statements over the past year, the purpose of an Executive Order directed by the President can hardly be deemed speculative when the President himself has traveled the country telling us why he issued it. As the Fourth Circuit found, time and again President Trump has told the public that the Order exists to ban Muslims because they are a problem and they are not welcome here. Even as that message has come through loud and clear, on Twitter and at political rallies, virtually none of his statements have evinced concern for supposedly unique threats from the six Muslim-majority nations covered by the Order. His motives here are not inscrutable, as his lawyers have repeatedly (but implausibly) insisted.

Great mischief could follow from a holding that allowed the President to speak about the nature and purpose of his own executive orders without any legal consequence. If the President's words mean nothing to this Court—even as they mean everything to millions of people affected by his Order—then the rule of law may suffer. Indeed, if the Judiciary were to disregard President Trump's statements, the gap between lived reality and constitutional law would grow intolerably vast. As a matter of law and public legitimacy, it would be anomalous for this Court to test the constitutionality of the Order in a parallel reality, where statements broadcast (and tweeted) on a global stage are treated as non-existent.

This Court's decision will reverberate throughout American life. It will teach the people of this Nation—and migrants worldwide—about the meaning of freedom and the Constitution. If this Court upholds the Order, people of all faiths, but especially Muslims, will learn that the First Amendment permits the President to ban people from this Nation because he disapproves of their faith. Respectfully, that is not the law and this Court should not make it so.

Further, even if this Court were to conclude that national security concerns played some role in the Order's original enactment (and its baffling continuation over eight months later), that still would not save it. Animus may co-exist with legitimate motives. As this Court has explained, where the government acts on the basis of mixed motives, courts do not hesitate to invalidate official acts when animus was a *primary* or *essential* motive, as it was here.

In that respect, *Korematsu v. United States* (1944) is instructive. As *Korematsu* teaches, the combination of animus and an actual (or perceived) national security threat is uniquely toxic: a veneer of noble motive can be invoked to justify the most horrid abuses. Even if an official begins with some good intentions, animus corrupts and distorts any motive it touches. Here, only by ignoring months of clear and consistent statements by the President could it be thought that he did not act on the basis of animus toward Muslims in following through on his promise to ban them from entering the United States. Not only did he ban many Muslims from entering the nation, but he has also repeatedly made anti-Muslim claims inflicting stigma and disability on Muslims nationwide. While the President often enjoys a presumption of regularity, here that presumption is rebutted by myriad instances of irregularity that comprise an assault on religious liberty in America.

In 1785, James Madison warned against any law departing "from that generous policy, which, offering an Asylum to the persecuted and oppressed of every Nation and Religion, promised a lustre to our country, and an accession to the number of its citizens." He added:

> Instead of holding forth an Asylum to the persecuted, [the Bill] is itself a signal of persecution. It degrades from the equal rank of Citizens all those whose opinions in Religion do not bend to those of the Legislative authority. Distant as it may be in its present form from the Inquisition, it differs from it only in degree. The one is the first step, the other the last in the career of intolerance. The magnanimous sufferer under this cruel scourge in foreign Regions, must view the Bill as a Beacon on our Coast, warning him to seek some other haven, where liberty and philanthropy in their due extent, may offer a more certain repose from his Troubles.

The bill against which Madison remonstrated has been consigned to the dustbin of history. But the underlying evils against which Madison warned are still with us. This case does not present them in disguise. No, "this wolf comes as a wolf." President Trump has repeatedly expressed the animus that motivated his promises, and subsequent acts, to ban persons of a single faith from entering the United States. For religious liberty to endure, the Order must be enjoined. . . .

Dissenting Opinion in
Trump v. Hawaii
by Justice Sonia Sotomayor (2018)

> *In the ultimate Supreme Court case addressing the legal brief submitted above, the majority rejected the claim that the travel ban was in violation of the Establishment Clause, finding that it did not exceed executive power in the field of immigration. However, the dissent by Justice Sotomayor argues that the travel ban was illicitly motivated by religious animus.*

Justice Sotomayor, with whom Justice Ginsburg joins, dissenting.

The United States of America is a Nation built upon the promise of religious liberty. Our Founders honored that core promise by embedding the principle of religious neutrality in the First Amendment. The Court's decision today fails to safeguard that fundamental principle. It leaves undisturbed a policy first advertised openly and unequivocally as a "total and complete shutdown of Muslims entering the United States" because the policy now masquerades behind a façade of national-security concerns. But this repackaging does little to cleanse Presidential Proclamation No. 9645 of the appearance of discrimination that the President's words have created. Based on the evidence in the record, a reasonable observer would conclude that the Proclamation was motivated by anti-Muslim animus. That alone suffices to show that plaintiffs are likely to succeed on the merits of their Establishment Clause claim. The majority holds otherwise by ignoring the facts, misconstruing our legal precedent, and turning a blind eye to the pain and suffering the Proclamation inflicts upon countless families and individuals, many of whom are United States citizens. Because that troubling result runs contrary to the Constitution and our precedent, I dissent.

I

Plaintiffs challenge the Proclamation on various grounds, both statutory and constitutional. . . . Whatever the merits of plaintiffs' complex statutory claims, the Proclamation must be enjoined for a more fundamental reason: It runs afoul of the Establishment Clause's guarantee of religious neutrality.

A

The Establishment Clause forbids government policies "respecting an establishment of religion." The "clearest command" of the Establishment Clause is that the Government cannot favor or disfavor one religion over another. Consistent with that clear command, this Court has long acknowledged that governmental actions that favor one religion "inevitabl[y]" foster "the hatred, disrespect and even contempt of those who [hold] contrary beliefs." That is so, this Court has held, because such acts send messages to members of minority faiths "'that they are outsiders, not full members of the political community.'" To guard against this serious harm, the Framers mandated a strict "principle of denominational neutrality."

. . . To determine whether plaintiffs have proved an Establishment Clause violation, the Court asks whether a reasonable observer would view the government action as enacted for the purpose of disfavoring a religion.

In answering that question, this Court has generally considered the text of the government policy, its operation, and any available evidence regarding "the historical background of the decision under challenge, the specific series of events leading to the enactment or official policy in question, and the legislative or administrative history, including contemporaneous statements made by" the decisionmaker. At the same time, however, courts must take care not to engage in "any judicial psychoanalysis of a drafter's heart of hearts."

B

1

Although the majority briefly recounts a few of the statements and background events that form the basis of plaintiffs' constitutional challenge, that highly abridged account does not tell even half of the story. The full record paints a far more harrowing picture, from which a reasonable observer would readily conclude that the Proclamation was motivated by hostility and animus toward the Muslim faith.

During his Presidential campaign, then-candidate Donald Trump pledged that, if elected, he would ban Muslims from entering the United States. Specifically, on December 7, 2015, he issued a formal statement "calling for a total and complete shutdown of Muslims entering the United States." . . .

On December 8, 2015, Trump justified his proposal during a television interview by noting that President Franklin D. Roosevelt "did the same thing" with respect to the internment of Japanese Americans during World War II. In January 2016, during a Republican primary debate, Trump was asked whether he wanted to "rethink [his] position" on "banning Muslims from entering the country." He answered, "No." A month later, at a rally in South Carolina, Trump told an apocryphal story about United States General John J. Pershing killing a large group of Muslim insurgents in the Philippines with bullets dipped in pigs' blood in the early 1900's. In March 2016, he expressed his belief that "Islam hates us. . . . [W]e can't allow people coming into this country who have this hatred of the United States . . . [a]nd of people that are not Muslim." That same month, Trump asserted that "[w]e're having problems with the Muslims, and we're having problems with Muslims coming into the country." He therefore called for surveillance of mosques in the United States, blaming terrorist attacks on Muslims' lack of "assimilation" and their commitment to "sharia law." A day later, he opined that Muslims "do not respect us at all" and "don't respect a lot of the things that are happening throughout not only our country, but they don't respect other things."

As Trump's presidential campaign progressed, he began to describe his policy proposal in slightly different terms. In June 2016, for instance, he characterized the policy proposal as a suspension of immigration from countries "where there's a proven history of terrorism." He also described the proposal as rooted in the need to stop "importing radical Islamic terrorism to the West through a failed immigration system." Asked in July 2016 whether he was "pull[ing] back from" his pledged Muslim ban, Trump responded, "I actually don't think it's a rollback. In fact, you could say it's an expansion." He then explained that he used different terminology because "[p]eople were so upset when [he] used the word Muslim." . . .

On January 27, 2017, one week after taking office, President Trump signed Executive Order No. 13769, entitled "Protecting the Nation from Foreign Terrorist Entry into the United States." As he signed it, President Trump read the title, looked up, and said "We all know what that means." That same day, President Trump explained to the media that, under EO–1, Christians would be given priority for entry as refugees into the United States. In particular, he bemoaned the fact that in the past, "[i]f you were a Muslim [refugee from Syria] you could come in, but if you were a Christian, it was almost impossible." Considering that past policy "very unfair," President Trump explained that EO–1 was designed "to help" the Christians in Syria. The following day, one of President Trump's key advisers candidly drew the connection between EO–1 and the "Muslim ban" that the President had pledged to implement if elected. According to that adviser, "[W]hen [Donald Trump] first announced it, he said, 'Muslim ban.' He called me up. He said, 'Put a commission together. Show me the right way to do it legally.'" . . .

On March 6, 2017, President Trump issued that new executive order, which, like its predecessor, imposed temporary entry and refugee bans. One of the President's senior advisers publicly explained that EO–2 would "have the same basic policy outcome" as EO–1, and that any changes would address "very technical issues that were brought up by the court." After EO–2 was issued, the White House Press Secretary told reporters that, by issuing EO–2, President Trump "continue[d] to deliver on . . . his most significant campaign promises." That statement was consistent with President Trump's own declaration that "I keep my campaign promises, and our citizens will be very happy when they see the result."

Before EO–2 took effect, federal District Courts in Hawaii and Maryland enjoined the order's travel and refugee bans. . . .

While litigation over EO–2 was ongoing, President Trump repeatedly made statements alluding to a desire to keep Muslims out of the country. . . .

In September 2017, President Trump tweeted that "[t]he travel ban into the United States should be far larger, tougher and more specific—but stupidly, that would not be politically correct!" Later that month, on September 24, 2017, President Trump issued Presidential Proclamation No. 9645, which restricts entry of certain nationals from six Muslim-majority countries. On November 29, 2017, President Trump "retweeted" three anti-Muslim videos, entitled "Muslim Destroys a Statue of Virgin Mary!", "Islamist mob pushes teenage boy off roof and beats him to death!", and "Muslim migrant beats up Dutch boy on crutches!" Those videos were initially tweeted by a British political party whose mission is to oppose "all alien and destructive politic[al] or religious doctrines, including . . . Islam." When asked about these videos, the White House Deputy Press Secretary connected them to the Proclamation, responding that the "President has been talking about these security issues for years now, from the campaign trail to the White House" and "has addressed these issues with the travel order that he issued earlier this year and the companion proclamation." . . .

2

Taking all the relevant evidence together, a reasonable observer would conclude that the Proclamation was driven primarily by anti-Muslim animus, rather than by the Government's asserted national-security justifications. . . .

Moreover, despite several opportunities to do so, President Trump has never disavowed any of his prior statements about Islam. Instead, he has continued to make remarks that a reasonable observer would view as an unrelenting attack on the Muslim religion and its followers. Given President Trump's failure to correct the reasonable perception of his apparent hostility toward the Islamic faith, it is unsurprising that the President's lawyers have, at every step in the lower courts, failed in their attempts to launder the Proclamation of its discriminatory taint. . . .

II

The majority first emphasizes that the Proclamation "says nothing about religion." Even so, the Proclamation, just like its predecessors, overwhelmingly targets Muslim-majority nations. Given the record here, including all the President's statements linking the Proclamation to his apparent hostility toward Muslims, it is of no moment that the Proclamation also includes minor restrictions on two non-Muslim majority countries, North Korea and Venezuela, or that the Government has removed a few Muslim-majority countries from the list of covered countries since EO–1 was issued. Consideration of the entire record supports the conclusion that the inclusion of North Korea and Venezuela, and the removal of other countries, simply reflect subtle efforts to start "talking territory instead of Muslim," precisely so the Executive Branch could evade criticism or legal consequences for the Proclamation's otherwise clear targeting of Muslims. The Proclamation's effect on North Korea and Venezuela, for example, is insubstantial, if not entirely symbolic. A prior sanctions order already restricts entry of North Korean nationals, and the Proclamation targets only a handful of Venezuelan government officials and their immediate family members. As such, the President's inclusion of North Korea and Venezuela does little to mitigate the anti-Muslim animus that permeates the Proclamation.

The majority next contends that the Proclamation "reflects the results of a worldwide review process undertaken by multiple Cabinet officials." . . .

But, . . . the worldwide review does little to break the clear connection between the Proclamation and the President's anti-Muslim statements. For "[n]o matter how many officials affix their names to it, the Proclamation rests on a rotten foundation." The President campaigned on a promise to implement a "total and complete shutdown of Muslims" entering the country, translated that campaign promise into a concrete policy, and made several statements linking that policy (in its various forms) to anti-Muslim animus.

Ignoring all this, the majority empowers the President to hide behind an administrative review process that the Government refuses to disclose to the public. . . . Furthermore, evidence of which we can take judicial notice indicates that the multiagency review process could not have been very thorough. Ongoing litigation under the Freedom of Information Act shows that the September 2017 report the Government produced after its review process was a mere 17 pages. That the Government's analysis of the vetting practices of hundreds of countries boiled down to such a short document raises serious questions about the legitimacy of the President's proclaimed national-security rationale.

Beyond that, Congress has already addressed the national-security concerns supposedly undergirding the Proclamation through an "extensive and complex" framework governing "immigration and alien status." The Immigration and Nationality Act sets forth, in painstaking detail, a reticulated scheme regulating the admission of individuals to the United States. . . .

. . . Congress has already erected a statutory scheme that fulfills the putative national-security interests the Government now puts forth to justify the Proclamation. Tellingly, the Government remains wholly unable to articulate any credible national-security interest that would go unaddressed by the current statutory scheme absent the Proclamation. The Government also offers no evidence that this current vetting scheme, which involves a highly searching consideration of individuals required to obtain visas for entry into the United States and a highly searching consideration of which countries are eligible for inclusion in the Visa Waiver Program, is inadequate to achieve the Proclamation's proclaimed objectives of "preventing entry of nationals who cannot be adequately vetted and inducing other nations to improve their [vetting and information-sharing] practices."

For many of these reasons, several former national-security officials from both political parties—including former Secretary of State Madeleine Albright, former State Department Legal Adviser John Bellinger III, former Central Intelligence Agency Director John Brennan, and former Director of National Intelligence James Clapper—have advised that the Proclamation and its predecessor orders "do not advance the national-security or foreign policy interests of the United States, and in fact do serious harm to those interests." . . .

In sum, none of the features of the Proclamation highlighted by the majority supports the Government's claim that the Proclamation is genuinely and primarily rooted in a legitimate national-security interest. What the unrebutted evidence actually shows is that a reasonable observer would conclude, quite easily, that the primary purpose and function of the Proclamation is to disfavor Islam by banning Muslims from entering our country.

III

As the foregoing analysis makes clear, plaintiffs are likely to succeed on the merits of their Establishment Clause claim. To obtain a preliminary injunction, however, plaintiffs must also show that they are "likely to suffer irreparable harm in the absence of preliminary relief," that "the balance of equities tips in [their] favor," and that "an injunction is in the public interest." Plaintiffs readily clear those remaining hurdles.

First, plaintiffs have shown a likelihood of irreparable harm in the absence of an injunction. As the District Court found, plaintiffs have adduced substantial evidence showing that the Proclamation will result in "a multitude of harms that are not compensable with monetary damages and that are irreparable—among them, prolonged separation from family members, constraints to recruiting and retaining students and faculty members to foster diversity and quality within the University community, and the diminished membership of the [Muslim] Association." . . .

Finally, plaintiffs and their *amici* have convincingly established that "an injunction is in the public interest." As explained by the scores of *amici* who have filed briefs in support of plaintiffs, the Proclamation has deleterious effects on our higher education system; national security; healthcare; artistic culture; and the Nation's technology industry and overall economy. . . .

IV

The First Amendment stands as a bulwark against official religious prejudice and embodies our Nation's deep commitment to religious plurality and tolerance. That constitutional promise is why, "[f]or centuries now, people have come to this country from every corner of the world to share in the blessing of religious freedom." Instead of vindicating those principles, today's decision tosses them aside. In holding that the First Amendment gives way to an executive policy that a reasonable observer would view as motivated by animus against Muslims, the majority opinion upends this Court's precedent, repeats tragic mistakes of the past, and denies countless individuals the fundamental right of religious liberty. . . .

Today's holding is all the more troubling given the stark parallels between the reasoning of this case and that of *Korematsu v. United States* (1944). In *Korematsu*, the Court gave "a pass [to] an odious, gravely injurious racial classification" authorized by an executive order. As here, the Government invoked an ill-defined national-security threat to justify an exclusionary policy of sweeping proportion. As here, the exclusion order was rooted in dangerous stereotypes about . . . a particular group's supposed inability to assimilate and desire to harm the United States. As here, the Government was unwilling to reveal its own intelligence agencies' views of the alleged security concerns to the very citizens it purported to protect. . . . And as here, there was strong evidence that impermissible hostility and animus motivated the Government's policy.

Although a majority of the Court in *Korematsu* was willing to uphold the Government's actions based on a barren invocation of national security, dissenting Justices warned of that decision's harm to our constitutional fabric. . . .

In the intervening years since *Korematsu*, our Nation has done much to leave its sordid legacy behind. . . . Today, the Court takes the important step of finally overruling *Korematsu*, denouncing it as "gravely wrong the day it was decided." This formal repudiation of a shameful precedent is laudable and long overdue. But it does not make the majority's decision here acceptable or right. By blindly accepting the Government's misguided invitation to sanction a discriminatory policy motivated by animosity toward a disfavored group, all in the name of a superficial claim of national security, the Court redeploys the same dangerous logic underlying *Korematsu* and merely replaces one "gravely wrong" decision with another.

Our Constitution demands, and our country deserves, a Judiciary willing to hold the coordinate branches to account when they defy our most sacred legal commitments. Because the Court's decision today has failed in that respect, with profound regret, I dissent.

Masterpiece Cakeshop, Ltd. v. Colorado Civil Rights Commission (2018)

> *In this high-profile case, a same-sex couple alleged that they had faced discrimination on the basis of their sexual orientation when a cake baker refused to make a cake for their wedding. The baker, who was a devout Christian, claimed that he had a free speech and free exercise right to refuse, as being compelled to provide the cake would violate his religious beliefs. Amid these competing claims, the Court wrote a narrow opinion: in Justice Kennedy's view, the Colorado Civil Rights Commission had shown animus toward the baker's religion in reviewing his case, which violated the requirement that the state be neutral toward religion.*

Justice Kennedy delivered the opinion of the Court. . . .

I

A

Masterpiece Cakeshop, Ltd., is a bakery in Lakewood, Colorado, a suburb of Denver. The shop offers a variety of baked goods, ranging from everyday cookies and brownies to elaborate custom-designed cakes for birthday parties, weddings, and other events.

Jack Phillips is an expert baker who has owned and operated the shop for 24 years. Phillips is a devout Christian. He has explained that his "main goal in life is to be obedient to" Jesus Christ and Christ's "teachings in all aspects of his life." And he seeks to "honor God through his work at Masterpiece Cakeshop." One of Phillips' religious beliefs is that "God's intention for marriage from the beginning of history is that it is and should be the union of one man and one woman." To Phillips, creating a wedding cake for a same-sex wedding would be equivalent to participating in a celebration that is contrary to his own most deeply held beliefs.

Phillips met Charlie Craig and Dave Mullins when they entered his shop in the summer of 2012. Craig and Mullins were planning to marry. At that time, Colorado did not recognize same-sex marriages, so the couple planned to wed legally in Massachusetts and afterwards to host a reception for their family and friends in Denver. To prepare for their celebration, Craig and Mullins visited the shop and told Phillips that they were interested in ordering a cake for "our wedding." They did not mention the design of the cake they envisioned.

Phillips informed the couple that he does not "create" wedding cakes for same-sex weddings. He explained, "I'll make your birthday cakes, shower cakes, sell you cookies and brownies, I just don't make cakes for same-sex weddings." The couple left the shop without further discussion.

The following day, Craig's mother, who had accompanied the couple to the cakeshop and been present for their interaction with Phillips, telephoned to ask Phillips why he had declined to serve her son. Phillips explained that he does not create wedding cakes for same-sex weddings because of his religious opposition to same-sex marriage, and also because Colorado (at that time) did not recognize same-sex marriages. He later explained his belief that "to create a wedding cake for an event that celebrates something that directly goes against the teachings of the Bible, would have been a personal endorsement and participation in the ceremony and relationship that they were entering into."

B

For most of its history, Colorado has prohibited discrimination in places of public accommodation. In 1885, less than a decade after Colorado achieved statehood, the General Assembly passed "An Act to Protect All Citizens in Their Civil Rights," which guaranteed "full and equal enjoyment" of certain public facilities to "all citizens," "regardless of race, color or previous condition of servitude." A decade later, the General Assembly expanded the requirement to apply to "all other places of public accommodation."

Today, the Colorado Anti-Discrimination Act (CADA) carries forward the state's tradition of prohibiting discrimination in places of public accommodation. Amended in 2007 and 2008 to prohibit discrimination on the basis of sexual orientation as well as other protected characteristics, CADA in relevant part provides as follows:

"It is a discriminatory practice and unlawful for a person, directly or indirectly, to refuse, withhold from, or deny to an individual or a group, because of disability, race, creed, color, sex, sexual orientation, marital status, national origin, or ancestry, the full and equal enjoyment of the goods, services, facilities, privileges, advantages, or accommodations of a place of public accommodation."

The Act defines "public accommodation" broadly to include any "place of business engaged in any sales to the public and any place offering services . . . to the public," but excludes "a church, synagogue, mosque, or other place that is principally used for religious purposes." . . .

C

Craig and Mullins filed a discrimination complaint against Masterpiece Cakeshop and Phillips in August 2012, shortly after the couple's visit to the shop. The complaint alleged that Craig and Mullins had been denied "full and equal service" at the bakery because of their sexual orientation, and that it was Phillips' "standard business practice" not to provide cakes for same-sex weddings.

The Civil Rights Division opened an investigation. . . . The investigation found that Phillips had declined to sell custom wedding cakes to about six other same-sex couples on this basis. The investigator also recounted that, according to affidavits submitted by Craig and Mullins, Phillips' shop had refused to sell cupcakes to a lesbian couple for their commitment celebration because the shop "had a policy of not selling baked goods to same-sex couples for this type of event." Based on these findings, the Division found probable cause

that Phillips violated CADA and referred the case to the
Civil Rights Commission. . . .

II

A

Our society has come to the recognition that gay persons and
gay couples cannot be treated as social outcasts or as inferior
in dignity and worth. For that reason the laws and the Constitution can, and in some instances must, protect them in the
exercise of their civil rights. The exercise of their freedom on
terms equal to others must be given great weight and respect
by the courts. At the same time, the religious and philosophical objections to gay marriage are protected views and in
some instances protected forms of expression. As this Court
observed in *Obergefell v. Hodges* (2015), "[t]he First Amendment ensures that religious organizations and persons are
given proper protection as they seek to teach the principles
that are so fulfilling and so central to their lives and faiths."
Nevertheless, while those religious and philosophical objections are protected, it is a general rule that such objections do
not allow business owners and other actors in the economy
and in society to deny protected persons equal access to goods
and services under a neutral and generally applicable public
accommodations law. . . .

When it comes to weddings, it can be assumed that a
member of the clergy who objects to gay marriage on moral
and religious grounds could not be compelled to perform the
ceremony without denial of his or her right to the free exercise of religion. This refusal would be well understood in our
constitutional order as an exercise of religion, an exercise that

gay persons could recognize and accept without serious diminishment to their own dignity and worth. Yet if that exception were not confined, then a long list of persons who provide goods and services for marriages and weddings might refuse to do so for gay persons, thus resulting in a community-wide stigma inconsistent with the history and dynamics of civil rights laws that ensure equal access to goods, services, and public accommodations.

It is unexceptional that Colorado law can protect gay persons, just as it can protect other classes of individuals, in acquiring whatever products and services they choose on the same terms and conditions as are offered to other members of the public. And there are no doubt innumerable goods and services that no one could argue implicate the First Amendment. Petitioners conceded, moreover, that if a baker refused to sell any goods or any cakes for gay weddings, that would be a different matter and the State would have a strong case under this Court's precedents that this would be a denial of goods and services that went beyond any protected rights of a baker who offers goods and services to the general public and is subject to a neutrally applied and generally applicable public accommodations law.

Phillips claims, however, that a narrower issue is presented. He argues that he had to use his artistic skills to make an expressive statement, a wedding endorsement in his own voice and of his own creation. As Phillips would see the case, this contention has a significant First Amendment speech component and implicates his deep and sincere religious beliefs. In this context the baker likely found it difficult to find a line where the customers' rights to goods and services became a demand for him to exercise the right of his own personal expression for their message, a message he could not express in a way consistent with his religious beliefs.

Phillips' dilemma was particularly understandable given the background of legal principles and administration of the law in Colorado at that time. His decision and his actions leading to the refusal of service all occurred in the year 2012. At that point, Colorado did not recognize the validity of gay marriages performed in its own State. At the time of the events in question, this Court had not issued its decisions either in *United States v. Windsor* (2013), or *Obergefell*. Since the State itself did not allow those marriages to be performed in Colorado, there is some force to the argument that the baker was not unreasonable in deeming it lawful to decline to take an action that he understood to be an expression of support for their validity when that expression was contrary to his sincerely held religious beliefs, at least insofar as his refusal was limited to refusing to create and express a message in support of gay marriage, even one planned to take place in another State.

At the time, state law also afforded storekeepers some latitude to decline to create specific messages the storekeeper considered offensive. Indeed, while enforcement proceedings against Phillips were ongoing, the Colorado Civil Rights Division itself endorsed this proposition in cases involving other bakers' creation of cakes, concluding on at least three occasions that a baker acted lawfully in declining to create cakes with decorations that demeaned gay persons or gay marriages.

There were, to be sure, responses to these arguments that the State could make when it contended for a different result in seeking the enforcement of its generally applicable state regulations of businesses that serve the public. And any decision in favor of the baker would have to be sufficiently constrained, lest all purveyors of goods and services who object to gay marriages for moral and religious reasons in effect be allowed to put up signs saying "no goods or services will be sold if they will be used for gay marriages," something that would impose a serious stigma on gay persons. But, nonetheless, Phillips was entitled to the neutral and respectful consideration of his claims in all the circumstances of the case.

B

The neutral and respectful consideration to which Phillips was entitled was compromised here, however. The Civil Rights Commission's treatment of his case has some elements of a clear and impermissible hostility toward the sincere religious beliefs that motivated his objection.

That hostility surfaced at the Commission's formal, public hearings, as shown by the record. On May 30, 2014, the seven-member Commission convened publicly to consider Phillips' case. At several points during its meeting, commissioners endorsed the view that religious beliefs cannot legitimately be carried into the public sphere or commercial domain, implying that religious beliefs and persons are less than fully welcome in Colorado's business community. One commissioner suggested that Phillips can believe "what he wants to believe," but cannot act on his religious beliefs "if he decides to do business in the state." A few moments later, the commissioner restated the same position: "[I]f a businessman wants to do business in the state and he's got an issue with the—the law's impacting his personal belief system, he needs to look at being able to compromise." Standing alone, these statements are susceptible of different interpretations. On the one hand, they might mean simply that a business cannot refuse to provide services based on sexual orientation, regardless of the proprietor's personal views. On the other hand, they might be seen as inappropriate and dismissive comments showing lack of due consideration for Phillips' free exercise rights and the dilemma he faced. In view of the comments that followed, the latter seems the more likely.

On July 25, 2014, the Commission met again. This meeting, too, was conducted in public and on the record. On this occasion another commissioner made specific reference to the previous meeting's discussion but said far more to disparage Phillips' beliefs. The commissioner stated:

"I would also like to reiterate what we said in the hearing or the last meeting. Freedom of religion and religion has been used to justify all kinds of discrimination throughout history, whether it be slavery, whether it be the holocaust, whether it be—I mean, we—we can list hundreds of situations where freedom of religion has been used to justify discrimination. And to me it is one of the most despicable pieces of rhetoric that people can use to—to use their religion to hurt others."

To describe a man's faith as "one of the most despicable pieces of rhetoric that people can use" is to disparage his religion in at least two distinct ways: by describing it as despicable, and also by characterizing it as merely rhetorical—something insubstantial and even insincere. The commissioner even went so far as to compare Phillips' invocation of his sincerely held religious beliefs to defenses of slavery and the Holocaust. This sentiment is inappropriate for a Commission charged with the solemn responsibility of fair and neutral enforcement of Colorado's antidiscrimination law—a law that protects discrimination on the basis of religion as well as sexual orientation.

The record shows no objection to these comments from other commissioners. And the later state-court ruling reviewing the Commission's decision did not mention those comments, much less express concern with their content.

Nor were the comments by the commissioners disavowed in the briefs filed in this Court. For these reasons, the Court cannot avoid the conclusion that these statements cast doubt on the fairness and impartiality of the Commission's adjudication of Phillips' case. . . .

Another indication of hostility is the difference in treatment between Phillips' case and the cases of other bakers who objected to a requested cake on the basis of conscience and prevailed before the Commission.

As noted above, on at least three other occasions the Civil Rights Division considered the refusal of bakers to create cakes with images that conveyed disapproval of same-sex marriage, along with religious text. Each time, the Division found that the baker acted lawfully in refusing service. It made these determinations because, in the words of the Division, the requested cake included "wording and images [the baker] deemed derogatory."

The treatment of the conscience-based objections at issue in these three cases contrasts with the Commission's treatment of Phillips' objection. The Commission ruled against Phillips in part on the theory that any message the requested wedding cake would carry would be attributed to the customer, not to the baker. Yet the Division did not address this point in any of the other cases with respect to the cakes depicting anti-gay marriage symbolism. . . .

A principled rationale for the difference in treatment of these two instances cannot be based on the government's own assessment of offensiveness. Just as "no official, high or petty, can prescribe what shall be orthodox in politics, nationalism, religion, or other matters of opinion," it is not, as the Court has repeatedly held, the role of the State or its officials to prescribe what shall be offensive. . . .

C

For the reasons just described, the Commission's treatment of Phillips' case violated the State's duty under the First Amendment not to base laws or regulations on hostility to a religion or religious viewpoint. . . .

. . . The Free Exercise Clause bars even "subtle departures from neutrality" on matters of religion. Here, that means the Commission was obliged under the Free Exercise Clause to proceed in a manner neutral toward and tolerant of Phillips' religious beliefs. The Constitution "commits government itself to religious tolerance, and upon even slight suspicion that proposals for state intervention stem from animosity to religion or distrust of its practices, all officials must pause to remember their own high duty to the Constitution and to the rights it secures."

Factors relevant to the assessment of governmental neutrality include "the historical background of the decision under challenge, the specific series of events leading to the enactment or official policy in question, and the legislative or administrative history, including contemporaneous statements made by members of the decisionmaking body." In view of these factors the record here demonstrates that the Commission's consideration of Phillips' case was neither tolerant nor respectful of Phillips' religious beliefs. . . . It hardly requires restating that government has no role in deciding or even suggesting whether the religious ground for Phillips' conscience-based objection is legitimate or illegitimate. On these facts, the Court must draw the inference that Phillips' religious objection was not considered with the neutrality that the Free Exercise Clause requires. . . .

III

The Commission's hostility was inconsistent with the First Amendment's guarantee that our laws be applied in a manner that is neutral toward religion. Phillips was entitled to a neutral decisionmaker who would give full and fair consideration to his religious objection as he sought to assert it in all of the circumstances in which this case was presented, considered, and decided. In this case the adjudication concerned a context that may well be different going forward in the respects noted above. However later cases raising these or similar concerns are resolved in the future, for these reasons the rulings of the Commission and of the state court that enforced the Commission's order must be invalidated.

The outcome of cases like this in other circumstances must await further elaboration in the courts, all in the context of recognizing that these disputes must be resolved with tolerance, without undue disrespect to sincere religious beliefs, and without subjecting gay persons to indignities when they seek goods and services in an open market.

The judgment of the Colorado Court of Appeals is reversed.

It is so ordered.

Acknowledgments

I would like to thank all of the people who have helped bring this series and volume to life by reading drafts, providing edits, and helping to put together the final versions. Aidan Calvelli provided careful editing and thoughtful input on all aspects of the series. Priyanka Podugu brought a keen eye to helping me compile materials, highlighting selections that brought out the key themes of liberty. My wife, Allison Brettschneider, was, as she always is, an invaluable partner in this work, giving substantive editorial feedback. Nelson Tebbe and Micah Schwartzman provided important input for this volume. David McNamee and Kevin McGravey graciously read drafts and provided valuable comments and suggestions. I would also like to thank Elda Rotor and Elizabeth Vogt from Penguin for all they have done to make this series possible, and Rafe Sagelyn, my agent, for his continued support, encouragement, and guidance.

Unabridged Source Materials

PART I

Roger Williams, "A Plea for Religious Liberty," 1644. https://www.digitalhistory.uh.edu/disp_textbook.cfm?smtID=3&psid=1358.

John Locke, "A Letter Concerning Toleration," Liberty Fund, 1689. https://oll.libertyfund.org/title/goldie-a-letter-concerning-toleration-and-other-writings.

James Madison, "Memorial and Remonstrance against Religious Assessments," Founders Online, National Archives, 1785. https://founders.archives.gov/documents/Madison/01-08-02-0163.

Thomas Jefferson, "The Virginia Statute for Religious Freedom," January 16, 1786. https://www.digitalhistory.uh.edu/disp_textbook.cfm?smtID=3&psid=1357.

First Amendment to the United States Constitution, ratified in 1791.

PART II

George Washington, "Letter to Touro Synagogue," August 21, 1790. https://www.tourosynagogue.org/history-learning/gw-letter.

Thomas Jefferson, "Letter to the Danbury Baptists," Library of Congress, January 1, 1802. https://www.loc.gov/loc/lcib/9806/danpre.html.

James Madison, "Veto Act on Incorporating the Alexandria Protestant Episcopal Church," UVA Miller Center, February 21, 1811. https://millercenter.org/the-presidency/presidential-speeches/february-21-1811-veto-act-incorporating-alexandria-protestant.

James Madison, "Veto Message on Act of Relief for the Baptist Church," February 28, 1811. https://www.presidency.ucsb.edu/documents/veto-message-167.

Lemon v. Kurtzman, 403 U.S. 602 (1971).

Lynch v. Donnelly, 465 U.S. 668 (1984).

County of Allegheny v. American Civil Liberties Union, Greater Pittsburgh Chapter, 492 U.S. 573 (1989).

Town of Greece v. Galloway, 572 U.S. 565 (2014).

American Legion v. American Humanist Association, 588 U.S. __ (2019).

PART III

Sherbert v. Verner, 374 U.S. 398 (1963).

Employment Division, Department of Human Resources of Oregon v. Smith, 494 U.S. 872 (1990).

Church of the Lukumi Babalu Aye, Inc. v. City of Hialeah, 508 U.S. 520 (1993).

Burwell v. Hobby Lobby Stores, 573 U.S. 682 (2014).

Holt v. Hobbs, 574 U.S. 352 (2015).

PART IV

George W. Bush, "'Islam Is Peace' Says President," White House Archives, September 17, 2001. https://georgewbush-whitehouse.archives.gov/news/releases/2001/09/20010917-11.html.

Barack Obama, "A More Perfect Union," *The Washington Post*, March 18, 2008. https://www.washingtonpost.com/wp-dyn /content/article/2008/03/18/AR2008031801081.html?sid =ST2008031801183.

Donald J. Trump, "Executive Order Protecting the Nation from Foreign Terrorist Entry into the United States," March 6, 2017. https://www.whitehouse.gov/presidential-actions/executive-order -protecting-nation-foreign-terrorist-entry-united-states-2.

Brief amicus curiae on behalf of Constitutional Law Scholars, *Trump v. Hawaii*, 585 U.S. __ (2018).

Trump v. Hawaii, 585 U.S. __ (2018) (Sotomayor, J., Dissent).

Masterpiece Cakeshop, Ltd. v. Colorado Civil Rights Commission, 584 U.S. __ (2018).